Extraterrestrial Life Galactic Humans

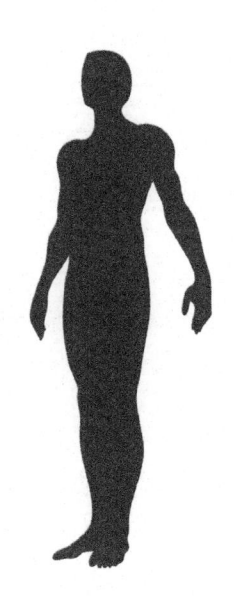

Jefferson Viscardi

Galactic Humans

© 2012 by Jefferson Viscardi and Rob Gauthier

All rights reserved. No part of this document may be reproduced or transmitted in any form or by any means, electronic, mechanical, photocopying, recording, or otherwise, without prior written permission of Jefferson Viscardi and Rob Gauthier.

Extraterrestrial Life
Galactic Humans

On the Plurality of Inhabited Worlds

Material channeled from
12 Galactic Humans through
Treb Bor yit-NE by Rob Gauthier

Questions developed and asked
by Jefferson Viscardi

Extraterrestrial Life

TABLE OF CONTENTS

FOREWORD..................09

PREFACE................... 17

RACE: MANILAH HUMANS
Chapter 1 - 08/23/2012............ 19
Planet Hadamanee; Average Lifespan: 500 years; Spokesperson: P't Leronee; Size: 5.5 feet; Age: 225 years old.

RACE: PLONO HUMANS
Chapter 2 - 08/23/2012............ 35
Planet: Plono; Average Lifespan: 1000 years; Spokesperson: Luhluprahkto; Height: 4 feet; Age: 586 years old.

RACE: ZANETLY HUMANS
Chapter 3 - 08/23/2012............ 53
Planet Zanetly; Average Lifespan: 2600 years; Spokesperson: Kroyzep; Height: 5.5 feet; Age: 1245 years old.

RACE: SANATI HUMANS
Chapter 4 - 08/23/2012............ 69
Planet Soldrantee; Average Lifespan: 1000 years; Spokesperson: Prontlasfornoplarecskitpla; Height: 5.5 feet; Age: 771 years old.

RACE: TRANKA HUMANS
Chapter 5 - 09/05/2012............................93
Nameless planet; Average Lifespan: 700 years;
Spokesperson: Haldra; Height: 6 feet; Age: 375 years old.

RACE: SAULOYD HUMANS
Chapter 6 - 09/05/2012............................113
Planet Sauloyd; Average Lifespan: 1250 years;
Spokesperson: Saul; Height: 7.6; Age: 971 years old.

RACE: DROHN-ONDAHG HUMANS
Chapter 7 - 09/06/2012............................137
Planet Drohn-ondahg; Average Lifespan: 1100 years;
Spokesperson: Mohj Ladrie; Height: 7 feet; Age: 444 years old.

RACE: KALAMEELO HUMANS
Chapter 8 - 09/06/2012............................157
Planet FramAnehl; Average Lifespan: 1500 years;
Spokesperson: Tassasol; Height: 2.5 feet; Age: 298 years old.

RACE: SUNAJE JEPILSO HUMANS
Chapter 9 - 09/07/2012............................177
Planet KissTorNaoh; Average Lifespan: 220 years;
Spokesperson: SunjilKajone; Height: 7.1 feet; Age: 111 years old.

RACE: SOLEPIONS HUMANS
Chapter 10 - 09/07/2012 205
Planet SolePions; Average Lifespan: 3000 years; Spokesperson: KwheelTravRiupaus; Height: 9.1 feet; Age: 1339 years old.

RACE: TIHNASTOLAH HUMANS
Chapter 11 - 09/12/2012 225
Planet Lahd-ieNacee; Average Lifespan: 600 years; Spokesperson: Iosoma; Height: 3.2 feet; Age: 243 years old.

RACE: SOWKWANTY HUMANS
Chapter 12 - 10/01/2012 249
Planet Kwiltar; Average Lifespan: 15000 years; Spokesperson: Dwantelgo; Height: 7.9 feet; Age: 5789 years old.

ABOUT THE AUTHORS 275

"PALPABLE" CURIOSITY 279

FOREWORD

THE DIFFERENT CATEGORIES OF INHABITED WORLDS

3. As a result of Spirit teaching, we know that the conditions of the various worlds differ one from the other, with respect to the degree of elevation or inferiority of their inhabitants, amongst whom are those inferior to the inhabitants of Earth, both physically and merrily; some in the same category, yet others which are more or less superior in every aspect.

In the inferior worlds, existence is all material, passions are sovereign and morality is almost nil. At the same time as the soul is progressing the material influences diminish, to such an extent that in the elevated worlds life is, by way of saying, all spiritual.

4. In the intermediate worlds good is mixed with evil, one or the other predominating according to the degree of advancement of the majority of the inhabitants. Although it is not possible to make an absolute classification of the different worlds, we can at least divide them in general terms by virtue of the state in which they are in, and the destiny they bring with them, based on the most predominant features upon each planet in the following manner: primitive worlds, destined to receive the initial incarnations of the human soul; worlds of tests and atonements, where evil predominates; regenerating worlds, where souls who still have to atone may absorb new strength by resting from the fatigue of fighting; blessed worlds, where goodness outweighs evil; celestial or divine worlds, inhabited by purified Spirits, where only goodness exists. Earth belongs to the category of worlds of tests and atonements, which is why mankind lives encompassed by

such misery.

5. Spirits who find themselves incarnated in any world are not bound to that same world indefinitely, nor do they go through all the phases of progress needed to achieve perfection in that one world. When they reach the maximum degree of advancement their world has to offer, they then pass on to a more elevated one, and so on successively till they reach the state of purified Spirits. These different worlds are stations where the Spirits find the elements they need for their progress that are in accordance to their degree of perfection. It is a recompense to ascend to a world of higher elevation, just as it is a punishment to prolong their stay in a miserable world, or to be relegated to another even more unhappy than the one they were for
ced to leave, due to persisting badness. (This is a summary of the teachings from all the Superior Spirits.)

NOTE: Excerpts from: KARDEC, Allan. The Gospel According to Spiritism. First Edition of this translation 1987. Printed by Masterprint. United Kingdom. Translated by J.A. Duncan. Original title 'L'Évangile Selon le Spiritisme' first published in France, 1864.

INSTRUCTIONS FROM THE SPIRITS SUPERIOR AND INFERIOR WORLDS

8. In qualifying inferior and superior worlds there is nothing absolute. A world is relatively inferior or superior only in relation to those other worlds which may be above or below it on the scale of progression.

In taking the Earth as a comparison, we may get an idea of what an inferior world is like by supposing us inhabitants to be similar to the primitive races or members of the barbaric nations, examples of which are still to be found amongst us today, these being the remnants of the primitive state of this planet. In the most backward worlds the inhabitants are, to a certain extent, rudimentary creatures, having human form but devoid of all beauty.

Their instincts have not yet softened to any sentiment of delicacy or benevolence, nor have they acquired any notions of justice or injustice. Brute force is the only known law. Without either industry or inventions, they pass their time in conquest of food. However, God does not abandon even one of His creatures; at the bottom of the darkest intelligence lurkes a seed, sometimes more, sometimes less developed, of a vague intuition of a supreme Being. This instinct is enough to make them superior one from the other and to prepare their ascension to a more complete life, for they are not degraded beings, but children who are growing.

In between the inferior and elevated levels are innumerable others. From the pure Spirits, dematerialised and brilliant with glory, it is impossible to recognise the primitive beings they once were, just as from the adult it is difficult to recognise the embryo.

9. In worlds which have reached a superior level, the moral and material stale is very different from that which exists on Earth.

As everywhere, the form is always human, but it is more beautiful, more perfected and above all else, purified. The body possesses nothing of the earthly materiality and consequently is not subject to the same necessities, sicknesses or deteriorations which the predominance of matter provokes. Due to the higher refinements, the senses are able to capture perceptions which the gross matter of this world obstructs. The specific lightness of body permits rapid and easy locomotion; instead of dragging painfully aver the ground the body floats, as it were, above the surface or glides through the air with no effort apart from that of desire, just as the angels are depicted as doing, or as the manes and the Elysian fields. According to his wishes Man keeps the features of his past migrations and shows himself to his friends as they knew him, except for the fact that he now radiates divine light, and is transfigured by interior impressions which are always of an elevated nature. In the place of countenances discoloured and dejected by suffering and passions, life and intelligence sparkle with splendour which painters have shown through the halo or aureole of the saints.

Very advanced Spirits suffer only slight resistance to matter, thus allowing body development to be extremely rapid, making infancy short and almost non-existent. With the absence of worry and anguish, life is proportionally longer than an Earth. In principle, longevity is in proportion the degree of advancement of each world. Death in no way conveys any horror of decomposition; far from causing terror, it is considered a happy transformation because there is no doubt as to the future. During life the soul, being no longer constricted by compact matter, expands
itself and delights in a lucidity which places it in an almost constant state of emancipation and allows completely free thought transmission.

10. In these blissful worlds relationships between peoples and individuals are always friendly, never perturbed by ambition to enslave their neighbour or make war. There are no masters nor slaves, none privileged by birth, only moral and intellectual

superiority which establishes all conditions and which ultimately gives supremacy. Authority receives and deserves the respect of everyone, as it is only given to those who merit it and is therefore always exercised with justice.

Man does not try to elevate himself above another but only above himself, by striving for perfection. His objective is to ascend to the category of pure Spirit, although this desire is never a torment but rather a noble ambition which induces him to study ardently in order to became an equal. In these worlds, all the delicate and elevated sentiments of human nature find themselves exalted and purified. Hate is unknown, as are petty jealousies and the covetous of envy. The ties of love and brotherhood hind all humanity each to the other so that the strong help the weak. Through a greater or lesser degree of intelligence, Man acquires possessions of a smaller or larger quantity. However, nobody suffers from want as no one needs to make atonement. In short, evil does not exist in these worlds.

11. Evil is still needed in your world in order to make known goodness; night in order to be able to admire light; sickness so as to be able to appreciate health. In those other worlds there is no need of these contrasts; eternal light, eternal beauty and eternal serenity of the soul offer proportional eternal happiness, free from the perturbations caused by the anguish of material life and the contact with evil creatures, who find no access to these realms. These are the things which cause the human Spirit most difficulty in understanding. Mankind has been sufficiently ingenious as to paint the torments of hell, but could never imagine the glories of Heaven. Why not? Because, being inferior, only pain and misery have been known and as yet the celestial brightness has never been seen, so one cannot speak of that which is unknown. However, while humanity is raising itself up and cleansing its soul, horizons are expanding and mankind begins to compare the goodness which is in front of him, as well as the badness which is behind him.

12. Meanwhile, the happy worlds are not specifically privileged orbs, as God is not partial to any one of His children. To

each one He gives the same rights and the same opportunities wherein to reach these worlds. He makes each one start at the same point and gives no one more than another. Even the highest categories are accessible to all. It only depends upon the individual to conquer their place by means of work, so reaching it more quickly or remaining inactive for centuries and centuries in the quagmire of humanity. (This is a summary of the teachings from all the Superior Spirits.)

NOTE: Excerpts from: KARDEC, Allan. The Gospel According to Spiritism. First Edition of this translation 1987. Printed by Masterprint. United Kingdom. Translated by J.A. Duncan. Original title 'L'Évangile Selon le Spiritisme' first published in France, 1864.

REGENERATING WORLDS

16. Among the many scintillating stars in the blue canopy of the sky, how many worlds there are like yours, destined by God to serve for atonement and probation! But although there are some that are more miserable, there are also others that are happier, like those of transition which can be called worlds of regeneration.

Each planetary vortex, moving in space round a common center, drags with it its own primitive worlds of exile, probation, regeneration and happiness. We have spoken to you of worlds where newly-born Spirits are placed, when they are still ignorant of both good and evil, but where they have the possibility of traveling towards God, being in possession of themselves through free-will. We have also revealed to you the fact that ample faculties are given to each soul to enable it to practice good. But alas, there are those who succumb!

So God, Who does not desire their annihilation, permits that they go to these worlds where from one incarnation to another they are purified and regenerated, returning worthy of the glory for which they were destined.

17. Regenerating worlds serve as transition phases between those of probation and happiness. The penitent soul finds calm and rest on them and can continue the purifying process.

Beyond doubt, Man still finds himself subject to the laws that rule matter: humanity still experiences your sensations and desires, but is liberated from the ungoverned passions to which you are slaves, freed from pride which silences the heart, envy which tortures and hate which suffocates. On all sides the word 'love' is written; perfect equity resides over all social relationships; everyone recognizes God and tries to travel in His direction by fulfilling His laws.

However, perfect happiness still does not exist in these worlds, only the dawning of happiness. There Man is still of flesh and blood, and because of this subject to vicissitudes from which only the completely dematerialized beings are liberated. He still has to suffer tests, although without the pungent anguishes of atonement. Compared to the Earth, these worlds are very pleasant, and many of you would be happy to inhabit them because they represent the calm after the storm, convalescence after cruel sickness.

Nevertheless, being less absorbed by material things, Man perceives the future better, comprehends the existence of other pleasures, promised by God to those who show themselves worthy when death has once again released them from their bodies in order to bestow upon them the true life. Free then, the soul hovers above all the horizons; no longer the feelings of gross matter, only the sensation of a pure and celestial perispirit absorbing emanations direct from God, in the fragrance of love and charity coming straight from His breast.

18. But alas! Man is still fallible even in these worlds and the spirit of evil has not completely lost its empire. Not to advance is to fall back, and if Man is not firmly placed along the pathway to righteousness he may return again to a world of atonement where new and more terrible tests await.

So at night, at the time of prayer and repose, contemplate the full canopy of the sky and the innumerable spheres which shine over your head, and ask yourself which ones lead to God and ask Him for one of these regenerating worlds to open to receive you after your atonement here on Earth. - SAINT AUGUSTIN (Paris, 1862).

NOTE: Excerpts from: KARDEC, Allan. The Gospel According to Spiritism. First Edition of this translation 1987. Printed by Masterprint. United Kingdom. Translated by J.A. Duncan. Original title 'L'Évangile Selon le Spiritisme' first published in France, 1864.

PREFACE

Now that you have a very good understanding about the progression of the soul through the process of a number of embodiments, to perfect itself morally and intellectually, (in planets that resonate with each individual's particular state of being), let us visit together some details as they are related to the story of this book.

It is known that I, Jefferson Viscardi, co-author with the medium Rob Gauthier, have this zest to understand and share my findings, about the subject hereby presented, in the purest possible way, with those who are as excited as I have always been to learn more about the variety of ways, shapes, places and times life can express itself.

Every serious student will by the force of reason and personal integrity neither criticize or judge haphazardly a material of this caliber. On the other hand, it would be immature and inconsequential for any of us to demand others to see what their inner eyes have yet not developed the necessary mechanisms to unveil. Many are not ready to see more than that which isn't necessarily in the purview of their field of action and reaction. To those, time will talk.

Through a process better known as psychophony where the entity "uses" the phonetic organs of the medium who is more or less unconscious during the channeling, depending on each individual and sometimes also on circumstances. I have spoken to Treb Bor yit-NE, through the mediumship of Rob. This fellow extraterrestrial being is an evolved soul embodied in a planet of love and light of reptlian humanoids. We have written a book with him and his society as well, so if you feel inclined to know more about him and his planet don't hesitate to look up: Benevolent Hybrid Reptilian Humans.

There are indeed too many inhabited worlds, schoolrooms to name or number and we have particularly focused on communicating with those who look primarily "exactly" like us and who exist spread out throughout this and other galaxies.

The human template (used by the souls to stage in each of these planets) have been perfected according to the collective level of spiritual growth and also the conditions presented by each planet mechanisms in what refers to the inner organs and reproduction rituals.

Presentations aside, Treb Bor yit-NE (who also functions in the capacity of a spiritual guide to the medium), have made the connections possible to each of the human races (all more advanced than our own). These benevolent beings, who so graciously agreed to donate a little of their time and wisdom in order to share with us what is life like in their planets, from where moral imbalances such as wrath, greed, sloth, pride, lust, envy, gluttony or any feeling of disconnection from self to others no longer plagues one's society.

I am delighted to preface to you this book as a victor who conquered the Everest mountain of extraterrestrial intelligent life research and I am sure my partner in service feels as excited. I am truly humbled for having "found favor" amongst these races to be worthy of their attention and object of their kindness. I am excited to be given the opportunity to know their processes and to be authorized to fully share what I heard and discovered, word by word, in this transcribed material with you and our world.

I wish you an unforgettable fulfilling journey of expansion from which there is usually, no return.

Jefferson Viscardi
October, 2012

MANILAH HUMANS

Chapter 1
08/23/2012

Planet Hadamanee
Lifespan: 500 years

Spokesperson: P't Leronee
Age: 225 years old

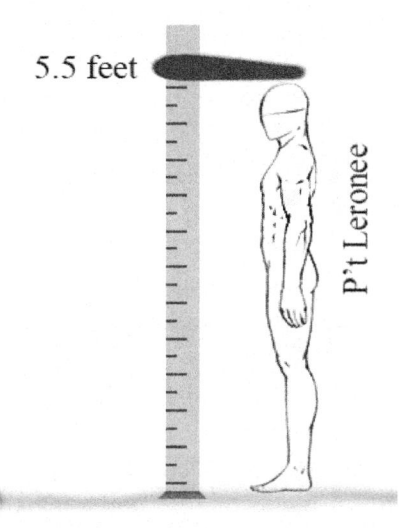

5.5 feet

P't Leronee

Future Human: Hello Jefferson.

Jefferson: Yes! Who are you?

Future Human: My name is P't Leronee

Jefferson: Where do you come from?

P't Leronee: I come from a system, a constellation that your race knows to be Cassiopeia.

Jefferson: Right. And what is the name of your planet?

P't Leronee: The name of the planet that we have is a name that is not translatable in your tongue but the best representation is Hadamanee.

Jefferson: Okay. And do you have a solar system like we do?

P't Leronee: No. It is quite different from yours. We have two stars, instead of one. Some of the planets that we have are around one. Some are around the other. And more are around both of them.

Jefferson: Wow. That is awesome. So, how many are around the first star?

P't Leronee: Well let's start from the smallest star. There are five planets on the smallest star. The smallest one is a class of star that your people call red dwarf. There are five planets on this. On the next star is one that is closer to the kind of star that you are from. Smaller, whitish-yellow start. Slightly smaller than yours. And around this one there are thirteen.

Jefferson: Wow. And which one is your planet with?

P't Leronee: I am one that is from a planet that goes around both stars. There are two of those.

Jefferson: Okay. I didn't know that. That is great. Wow. Why is it that the other planets don't go around two stars and these two go? Any special reason?

P't Leronee: No. It is only the way that the solar system is formed in the early environments. In the early environments there are some that were further out. One of the ones... the other one, not the one that we come from. But the other one was thrown out in a gravitational tug of war in an early environment from the star that is same as yours.

Jefferson: Thanks. What do you look like?

P't Leronee: We look very much like your race. The only difference is that our skin is very dark. In between... maybe the African tribes and perhaps, the Spanish people. Somewhere in between.

Jefferson: How long do you live in your physical body?

P't Leronee: About five hundred years.

Jefferson: And how old are you?

P't Leronee: I am two hundred and twenty three.

Jefferson: Oh okay. Understood. And what density are you guys in?

P't Leronee: We are one that has come over the forth threshold and we are starting to integrate more of the mind and consciousness into the fourth density. It is only been three generations since a full transition in the fourth density. So to what we understand to many other races that we meet is that we are still very young in this.

Jefferson: I see. What do you know about Earth?

P't Leronee: I know what I've heard from many other races. There are many Pleiadean members that always connect that are very similar to the way that we all look. We heard many rumors. Some of them... I am not very sure. Because when you look at a perspective you must see it within your own eyes. You cannot take another's viewpoint to be your truth. And this is why I have been very interested to speaking to you.

Jefferson: Wow. Thank you very much for coming forth to talk to us.

P't Leronee: Thank you for speaking to me and to the race as well.

Jefferson: How many people are there in your planet?

P't Leronee: About forty nine million.

Jefferson: That is not a lot. So is your planet as big as mine?

P't Leronee: Approximately half of the size of your planet from the understanding of how big it is.

Jefferson: Okay. And do you have government there?

P't Leronee: No. It is a society of sharing and giving others what they are in lack of. And it is a community. The word that your race would use to most accurately describe would be a communism... or a free trade... uh... trade is not the right word either...

Jefferson: I know a good name.

P't Leronee: Yes?

Jefferson: A resource based economy!

P't Leronee: That fits very well.

Jefferson: [Laughter] That is what we are looking to experience in our future if possible. [Giggles] Do you guys have sense of humor?

P't Leronee: Yeah. It is slightly different from yours. Our humor is based of enjoyment instead of wordplay, maybe. Perhaps because the language is so different.

Jefferson: Right. Are your constructions in any way similar to ours?

P't Leronee: The steel constructed places that you say are skyscrapers would be most accurately describing the complexity of the house. Even though we don't make it the same way. It is very similar to this. We are all living in two main areas of our planet. Altogether.

Jefferson: Oh I see. And... uh... For the education, how do you educate people?

P't Leronee: There is a set way. Once we are born, we are going through every family member that we have, connecting to them. Learning everything they have learned. And once twenty years is by, then we go to a center point in the town and we collect information from many people who are designated to teach it and once we do this, we learn very many things. For about ten years, or more. And after this, then we go to study whatever we wish to do for the rest of our race. Perhaps a specialty school... uh... is how you would see it.

Jefferson: And how are you born? Do you go over pregnancy like we do?

P't Leronee: Yes. It is exactly the same reproductive style that your race carries. Sexual activity, waiting for female to get birth after about two years, in the womb. It is approximately, two of your years. Once the child is born, it is born fairly small and it grows for some time. Probably it reaches full size at around thirty or thirty five years.

Jefferson: And does it stay around parents or does it belong to the community?

P't Leronee: It integrates with society as do we all. But it stays with its family for its whole life. In certain areas of the town are many... generations after generations of family and they all live in the same area and communicate. Family is something that we find very important to us. It is our tool of growth. Our family is what helps us understand the ways of our people and also the ways that are best to integrate our own consciousness with the rest of the planet. So important in this is to stay and remain with your family and to give them great love and spend great time with them.

Jefferson: How do you see the idea of God?

P't Leronee: We see... your thought on God is varying from different person to person but the majority sees it as a deity who is creating everything and is also controlling the destiny of one. This is an average perspective in your planet. If I am correct.

Jefferson: Well, go ahead... and how do you see?

P't Leronee: The way we see it is also a creator but it is not a complex personality. It is more of an energy. An energy of creation. Something that has great amounts of physical energy and disperses it all at once to be able to have many other smaller parts, connecting with each other to create more. And as this energy creates, it gives us our consciousness. It gives us our soul, it gives us our existence. But it doesn't dictate the values, ideas, working ethics or mindset of our people. What it does, it feeds us our own will to do so.

Jefferson: I see. And... uh... do you have competitions, sports?...

P't Leronee: We have various games. Competition isn't a proper word. We try to bring out the best in ourselves and by doing this we all compete with each other. But the idea of losing and winning... uh... even though it is a great idea to establish who is won. Who wins is not the important idea. It is how much you have been able to grow within one event or within one competition.

Jefferson: I see. Do you travel outside your planet?

P't Leronee: Yes we travel to many solar systems around our area but it is not as complex as some of the entities you've spoken to before. We are not at this point of consciousness yet. If we are being told correctly, this will happen soon. But we have to go through our growth and development before we get to this point.

Jefferson: So how do you travel far?

P't Leronee: We travel to other systems in crafts that we have manufactured. One that uses compressed air. Maybe nitrogen, oxygen... uh... one of these elements. I am not sure which is called in your race but it is compressed very highly and ignited. Not in a liquid form but in a compressed gas form.

Jefferson: What is your job in your race?

P't Leronee: For my job personally... it is to deliver things that people need. For instance if someone from the other town on the other side of our planet needs something, my job would be to take the transport and take as much of this as they need. If they are in need of a certain kind of food we would bring it to them. If they are in need of something else, we will bring it to them and they will bring it to us. Even though the towns are separated by a half of a planet, we are still very highly connected to all of them.

Jefferson: Why do you have to travel... doesn't technology take care of either creating things around them or to take care of the transportation itself?

P't Leronee: Well we have technology to take care of the needs that we have but we are also making these things. So when we are doing something that is of a specific uniqueness that they have not come around to getting that yet, then we will bring it to them.

Jefferson: So it is not like you bring them, either food or clothing...

P't Leronee: We can bring them food but it is usually food that is only available in our side of the planet.

Jefferson: Alright. And do you wear clothes?

P't Leronee: Oh yes. We wear garments that are made from a cloth from a small animal. I want to try to show you a similarity with your... uh... what is a worm that produces silk maybe? This would be the best but it is nothing like a worm. It is more like a smaller animal. I am trying to find much information in this man's head and it is a little hard to navigate this. Treb Bor yit-NE is helping me do this.

Jefferson: So, do men and women look the same? Like.. the hair?... do all have hair?, do all have five fingers?...

P't Leronee: Yes. In the majority or very small things as this, yes. We all have different features but yes all of the same body style, general height and build... very similar.

Jefferson: Do you get paid for your job?

P't Leronee: No. We do the job because we wish to help those who do not wish to do that, as they help us, as all of us help each other.

Jefferson: Have you been to Earth?

P't Leronee: No. That is a little outside. There has been farther travelings, than your planet. But it is usually done by other races that understand the further traveling. But there was no need ever to come to Earth. Even for those who are explorers of further areas... perhaps it wasn't in their interest to see your planet yet.

Jefferson: How did you get the invitation to share a message with us?

P't Leronee: There is an entity that you know as Treb Bor yit-NE that connects to a few of the people that lives here and there was an expression of someone who wanted to speak to Earth and many of us volunteered. But I was the first one.

Jefferson: Wow. Did you make a competition about who was going to talk?

P't Leronee: No. But if any more would have joined, I am sure they would have to find a better way. If more would have volunteered then perhaps we would have to have some sort of event for this.

Jefferson: How many volunteered?

P't Leronee: Around three or four thousands.

Jefferson: Wow. [Giggles] That is a lot. Why were you the first?

P't Leronee: I was there next to the man who made the announcement.

Jefferson: I see. So you raised your hand.

P't Leronee: Yes. I touched the man first and he understood that I wished to come and speak to you.

Jefferson: So, very good. I guess we are close to the time where you will be able to share with us your message. So feel free. Just so you know we are going to share this message with those who will find a way into it through law of attraction in order for us to learn from your race that is certainly more advanced than ours considering you already don't have wars anymore, you don't have a money society, you don't have government. I mean, by that alone we know you are much more advanced and that you can travel to other solar system too, indicates that. But yeah. It is used for us very important to hear what other races have to say and... uh... the floor is yours P't Leroneed.

P't Leronee: Thank you.

Jefferson: Please.

P't Leronee: To those of you on Earth who wish to listen; for those of you who are drawn here. There is a reason that you have come. It is become you are looking for growth. Most of you have many great understandings of the ideas that are shared. But some of you have a hard time finding the way to apply what you have learned into the momentum of your race. You are trying to find a way where your singular actions can affect all. I wish to let you understand that this is very possible by only doing what you need to inside. Many do not see that one action can affect many. But this is the way that it works, to our understanding. That once you have become at peace with yourself then you are able to be with peace at all that surround you.
    Once you become at peace with the local area of surroundings, you will be able to venture further out. Once you do this you will have an understanding and accepting towards all things that you come across. Whether it used to be good or bad or indifferent in your mind. Using this idea of the freedom to accept all things around you, you are able to move forward in a greater fashion. You can take ideas and use them in your life. But the point of your planet is that that our understanding is that you have trouble to apply these things. Well, if you have come this far, then obviously you are able to move forward. You would not have come to a place of this in your

consciousness unless you were able to accept certain ideas.

So, let us help you with certain ideas that we have for applying these things. For instance, the idea of judgment is something that we understand is very hard for your people to have, it is very hard to accept things that are not like you. From the understanding of Treb Bor yit-NE that even those who believe that they are very understanding in your race, still have ideas of being able to, not fully accept those who are not accepting. And this in itself is a judgment. You are judging those who can't accept others. This is still not a level that you can apply. So what you do is you take this mindset and place it in your front of the mind and when people talk to you and give you ideas that are different to you, collect these ideas and do not judge them. It is very important that you do not judge them. Place these ideas, all, at the front of your mind. And then give the idea or expression: if this is okay or good to me I would not have to have worried of it. If it was bad to me it would have repelled me from not being able to contact it or to come into connection with it.

So, what is it about my own thoughts and beliefs that can make this not appealing or different for me and study these ideas. We understand that you all have a meditative state that you use to try to connect to yourselves. Understanding this is very great. But also understand that this is only a toll. That once you come in line with what you truly are, as a human being, as a person from Earth, but more than that: the soul, you will be able to confront all of these things in a conscious mindset. One that places you able to walk from area to area and concern, determine... to make differences with these, differentiate the ideas that you have for what is good and bad, without having to go into the meditative state. There is a simple clue to what comes from places other than your heart. This is the struggle for you. If it gives any negative feelings, ones of fear, ones of anxiety then this is not a normal process of your soul. Remove this ideas and come to an understanding or peacefulness in your mind.

Once you have done this then you are able to accept the ideas of judging the ideas and the ideas of judging circumstances. Other ways to posses the idea of being able to apply thing is to be able to live every moment in happiness. If you are not doing this, then you are not applying the beliefs that you make, to believe that you are happy. When you say: I am a happy person because I have not done this or that or this but you don't seem to feel happy, then you are only fooling yourself into believing that your belief systems are not wrong. Judging these very harshly will still do you no good. When you look down on yourself in these ways it only brings more frustration and anger to you. So try to understand and not judge you on your own judgment. Even your own thoughts within this judgment. Using this will help you pursue true happiness within yourself.

Now, understanding that your planet goes through many hardships of war and financial means... this is something that you are trying to work out now. And this would appear to be why there is so much frustration amongst your people as a whole. Being tired of something and expressing it in a vocal manner or with your actions are the very first sign that you are really tired of something. So speaking of it, making actions on this, this shows that you are going in the right way. Act on the ideas of what you think is not right, is only adding to that in a way. If you try fight it head first, you are only bringing more fight within the battle. But when you look at it and you see it and you are tired of it and you make the changes in your mind of what not to do any longer and make that change, using the terminology that I have just explained, using that discernment process, then you area able to do it and not have a fight within you.

If you focus on worrying of these things too much, it will

tend to drawn your soul into the negative ideas and the negative energies that sometimes come with the releasing of the negative consciousness of a third density entity. And believe me. From generations back in stories that were handed down, spoken and written. This was not so long ago in our past that we were in this process as well. Fighting to be better and in this process seeing that we have fought to get better, and this is what have held us from progressing, this is what made the true change of our people. There has to be no fight. It is only a simple decision that puts you in whatever place that you wish to be. And I hope that you are able to encompass these ideas to you in your daily life and as a race in whole. Because we understand that if you were brought to us, it was for a reason. It was for the ability to connect that knowledge that we have to share with you. And I thank you so much.

Jefferson: So. Uh... Thank you very much for your sharing. I mean... the other thing that I wanted to ask before is... Are you in the future, what time line are you?

P't Leronee: We are approximately five hundred years or so in the future area.

Jefferson: Understood. And how tall are you?

P't Leronee: Five feet and a half.

Jefferson: Now, how do you feel now after you have spoken directly to a human being? And after having given us your message?

P't Leronee: I feel very happy and excited and grateful but I am still very curious to see certain aspects of humanity. Is there a way that I would be able to ask you a few questions?

Jefferson: Uh... Yes. There is. Well... Can I ask you to... I mean... if you can ask me one or two questions and then the other questions you have, if you could ask Treb, he knows everything about our planet. Because we have some time constraint and appointment with other races that also want to give us a message but by all means, you can... you can ask me... Ask me a couple of questions and then... uh... but then the other ones I'd really need you to ask Treb, or even we can arrange another session just for you to ask me questions. Because then we have another race. But go ahead.... what is...

P't Leronee: I will say this... that if you have trust that Treb Bor yit-NE has a complete comprehension of the ideology and your mindset as a race, then I will leave you to bear with your time constraints as you need.

Jefferson: Well you can ask... ask me one question then... the most... the most important, the most interesting for you. And then the rest...

P't Leronee: The most?

Jefferson: Yeah.

P't Leronee: The most interesting for me would be... How you are able to live in such high velocity changing of emotions of the ones around you. Even if you are not one that jumps from deep sadness to great happiness in short periods of time. How do you deal with others who do this?

Jefferson: Well, I think that... I will try to answer as short as I can, but... I think that the reason why we can do this is because we are moved by a feeling of brotherhood in a deeper sense.

Because down there, we know we are spirits; down there, we know we are immortal. And down there we all have a spirit guide whispering in our ears.

Even though most of us are not aware of that, we have a spirit guide showing us the way, whispering in our ears where to go, what to do and that in the end, no matter what the outcome is, everything is going to be great and everything is going to be alright. So with that we are able to trust, we are able to go through the difficulties of life and we are able to put out not only that the human race of Earth is strong in that sense but then, because we are, in this... one of the worst situations ever, other races can be too. [Giggles] That is it.

P't Leronee: This is the most beautifully put into a small group of words. I appreciated the energy within the words and the passion that you have. Thank you.

Jefferson: Fantastic. We are going to try and put this in the book too. So... uh... you share these ideas with your people yeah?

P't Leronee: Yes, thank you. We are very grateful.

Jefferson: Much love to you and thank you very much for coming forth.

P't Leronee: Thank you, you as well.

Jefferson: Thank you.

P't Leronee: Good bye.

Jefferson: Good bye.

Extraterrestrial Life

PLONO HUMANS
Chapter 2
08/23/2012

Planet: Plono
Lifespan: 1000 years.

Spokesperson: Luhluprahkto
Age: 586 years old

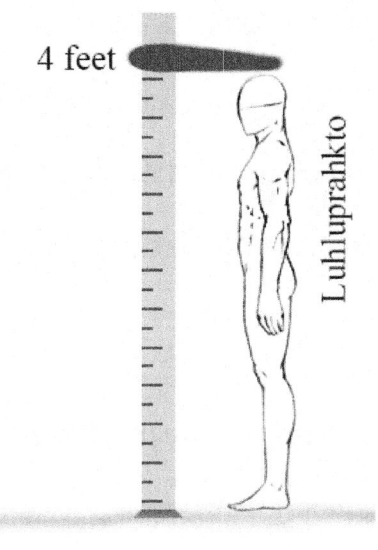

4 feet — Luhluprahkto

Galactic Human: Hello Jefferson!

Jefferson: Hey who are you?

Galactic Human: My name is Luhluprahkto

Jefferson: So what is your constellation?

Luhluprahkto: I am not sure... Give one second to reevaluate with Treb Bor yit-NE and I will see what he says.

***[Silence]

Jefferson: Thank you.

Luhluprahkto: He said it is in the leg of the Cannis Minor.

Jefferson: Okay and what is the name of your planet?

Luhluprahkto: The name name of our planet is Plono

Jefferson: Do you have a solar system like ours?

Luhluprahkto: It is not the same but it is very similar in the way that it is made of.

Jefferson: How many stars do you have?

Luhluprahkto: Just one!

Jefferson: How many planets do you have?

Luhluprahkto: We have six.

Jefferson: Which planet is yours?

Luhluprahkto: The fourth.

Jefferson: The fourth away from the Sun, right?

Luhluprahkto: Yes. Not from the opposite side.

Jefferson: Right. What do you look like?

Luhluprahkto: We are the same kind as you, the humanoid structure. We are around four feet tall. We have dark hair and we have very, very white skin. Not white like you guys think of white but more of the kind that might hurt your eyes if you look too long!

Jefferson: What is the color of your eyes?

Luhluprahkto: Green.

Jefferson: Is everybody like that?

Luhluprahkto: No. There are different kinds. There is green and blue... some have dark kind. Like dark, dark black.

Jefferson: Oh, I see. But the skin is the same color on everyone.

Luhluprahkto: Oh yes.

Jefferson: Okay and how long do you live in your physical body?

Luhluprahkto: It can be up to a thousand years, at times.

Jefferson: And how old are you?

Luhluprahkto: About five eighty six or eighty seven, maybe. In your years... about that.

Jefferson: And what density are you in?

Luhluprahkto: We are from fourth density from the way that you guys understand the densities. It is fourth.

Jefferson: Hmm. What do you know about Earth?

Luhluprahkto: We know that your race is pretty special for

many reasons. That you guys go crazy some times with each other and with other people. But for the most part you are pretty loving and you try to do things the right way. There are a lot of races that are watching for you guys now.

Jefferson: Wow. How many people are there in your planet?

Luhluprahkto: About a billion, maybe.

Jefferson: Wow. And is your planet as big as ours?

Luhluprahkto: Oh no. It is a little bit bigger. Probably about twice. Maybe two and a half.

Jefferson: And do you have governments?

Luhluprahkto: We have a society that is mostly of elders.

Jefferson: Oh do you mean that the elders organize the ways of distribution or that you don't have government to oversee that at all?

Luhluprahkto: Oh no. Those things aren't looked at. The elders are ones who help us. They guide us when we come to confrontational parts within our own journeys. Let's say I am going down the street and I don't know which way to go. So I would ask them. They just help us with our basic life issues.

Jefferson: Oh, I see. But that example is very simple because you usually follow your heart, right?

Luhluprahkto: Oh yes. That was just a joking around thing.

Jefferson: What was the last issue that you had to look for

elders, yourself?

Luhluprahkto: For me? Myself personally?

Jefferson: Yeah.

Luhluprahkto: I struggled with ideas of connecting to entities that some say could be negative. I understand that they are in the path that is their own way that is separate from the rest of connection but I feel the urge to help them and to reach out to them and even though I understand that is not what they want or need. I still feel propelled to do this. So I spoke to the elders about this and wanted to know what they thought.

Jefferson: And what did they say? No, no! No, no! No, no!

Luhluprahkto: No. They said that if I wished to reach out to them and if it was truly in my heart, to do what I wished to do. To try to help them but don't expect that they will embrace me. That they are in a separate path for a reason. The probability of me to even come into confrontation with them would be very small.

Jefferson: Hey what is the name of your race?

Luhluprahkto: The Plono.

Jefferson: Oh yeah, that is true. Yeah. Are your cities like ours?

Luhluprahkto: We have dwellings that are connected together. But nothing like a city. Maybe like a small village.

Jefferson: And transportation?

Luhluprahkto: We have various degrees of it. For our planet we have big things that carry lots of stuff at once. We've got smaller ones for our own personal needs. And then we have many... varieties of crafts that go outside of ours to other planets.

Jefferson: And these are powered by oil? Gasoline? Fossil fuel?

Luhluprahkto: Oh no. I understand that is a big thing with your race, but we use light. Light and transfer it into energy. Because the star that we are in is very bright.

Jefferson: Oh I see. And what about the education? How does that work?

Luhluprahkto: I don't think I understand the question.

Jefferson: How do you learn things?

Luhluprahkto: Uh... how do all things learn things?

Jefferson: [Laughter] Oh we go to classes!

Luhluprahkto: Oh. That is not the way we do. The way that we would do the similar learning. It is to be connected out to watch, to experience and try new things. And see what we like.

Jefferson: So do you stay with your family for how long? Or do you belong to the society? How does it work?

Luhluprahkto: We could do whichever. Whatever we feel is most in the heart to do.

Jefferson: Oh. Okay. So how are you guys born?

Luhluprahkto: It is a sexual thing, much as your race is. But we don't tend to have as long of periods that you hold on to them. So I think it is nine or ten months for your race, right?

Jefferson: Uh huh. Yes.

Luhluprahkto: Yeah. It is about half of that.

Jefferson: So you come out quick, huh?

Luhluprahkto: Oh yes.

Jefferson: And once you are born how long does it take for you to grow fully.

Luhluprahkto: Probably ninety... a hundred... a hundred and ten... depending on each individual.

Jefferson: Days right?

Luhluprahkto: What is this?

Jefferson: Probably ninety... a hundred to a hundred and ten days, right?

Luhluprahkto: Oh no. For a full size body in years. We are not very big when we are fully grown. So, there is a lot of growing. It is a very gradual thing.

Jefferson: Wow. So when you were thirty years old, how tall were you?

Luhluprahkto: About three, maybe three point one.

Jefferson: Oh okay. So you grow a lot initially and then you stick... you keep growing really, small amounts of size each season or whatever... [giggles]

Luhluprahkto: It is pretty quick at the beginning and then it is very, very well distributed, after.

Jefferson: Right. And are you in the future?

Luhluprahkto: Uh... in your time it is about a thousand years behind you.

Jefferson: Are you in the past?

Luhluprahkto: To your idea of time.

Jefferson: But you are more evolved than us.

Luhluprahkto: Oh yes. Uh... in technology basis? Oh yes.

Jefferson: How do you see God?

Luhluprahkto: That way that we see God is... uh... that one big creator... Huge! Not... uh... some people think in terms of never ending in size. But it is not that big. It is as big as all the universes put together. Which is still pretty big compared to what we are but this big God gives us all energy and it breaks it up into various amounts. We are not sure of the fraction but it is something that we keep working on, to see how many universes exactly. And once it breaks it down every universe... just like every cell in your body has a different function, so do those. So we are little cells in the big creator's body.

Jefferson: Wow. So he doesn't punish you or give you trinkets for Christmas?

Luhluprahkto: [Giggles] No. That is not what we do. No. It is... we are a function then, itself. Because we are a part of it and a specific module or specific breaking off point. The universe has its own function and we all do as we are supposed to, to gain the function to better the creator. Just like a cell.

Jefferson: Oh just to clarify. I am not making light of God. It is that some people's belief systems are such that make us... really... doubt if they are serious. Now... uh... (here on Earth it is just like that), but uh... okay. So do you pray to God?

Luhluprahkto: No. We connect to the highest thing that we can. Some of us connect to God quite frequently and we all do in a certain way by just going around day to day. Living on what we do. That is a kind of connection that is good enough.

Jefferson: So God is all in all.

Luhluprahkto: Yeah we are a part of it. And everything that is around is a smaller part of God's cellular breaking.

Jefferson: By the voice and speech pattern you seem to be a very happy person and have strong energy... by the way we talk... uh... why do you have that personality, any reason in particular?

Luhluprahkto: [Giggles] I am not sure of the exact reason but I like to be happy. This is just what we do.

Jefferson: Right, right. But I mean in a way that... you are like... ready, you seem to be going somewhere and really... uh... it seems you just drank coffee!

Luhluprahkto: [Giggles]

Jefferson: You are aware... you area awaken... you are lighten up! [Giggles]

Luhluprahkto: This is how our race functions. We are quite quick on the feet. We like to think fast, talk fast, move fast and the connection that I have with Treb is a very good one. He is a very old friend of mine.

Jefferson: Wow. Do you have competitions, sports, games?

Luhluprahkto: We have activities. But I don't think they are competitions or games. They are just activities that we all do together. Whatever the fun tend to be is what we are doing. For instance, forty or fifty years ago there was a big gathering at the water area and we were all throwing gigantic balls that have air in the middle and outside sacks are made or something almost like rubber to you and we are all bouncing back and forth to each other and that was very fun.

Jefferson: Wow. Do you have cats?

Luhluprahkto: No.

Jefferson: Oh anything close to that?

Luhluprahkto: No. The animals that we have are all air born animals.

Jefferson: Like... like... a flying cat.

Luhluprahkto: Uh... It is nothing like this... uh...

Jefferson: A bird then. A bird.

Luhluprahkto: Somewhat like that, it has the wings and then a long tail and it has four feet. So maybe it is a kind of cat.

Jefferson: [Laughter]

Luhluprahkto: I am not sure how you'd see it.

Jefferson: Do you guys travel outside of your planet?

Luhluprahkto: Oh yes. We travel very far.

Jefferson: How do you do that?

Luhluprahkto: We go into our crafts. The crafts that we use in the technology way... uh... we absorb much of the light and we have great storage systems for the energy at once and we are able to use that to start it and at once we go from there to where we need. It is kind of uh... an instant fashion... uh... when you are speaking to Treb Bor yit-NE, he describes an idea that you go and you can visit within your own traveling as an experience. This is the best that we are able to do. We have to hover through space many times to go from point a to b.

Jefferson: Oh I see. Okay. And what is your job in your race?

Luhluprahkto: We don't have a specific destination or a specific thing to do. We do whatever is helpful to others around us.

Jefferson: Are you aware of the race Plenatalaka?

Luhluprahkto: Uh... this is familiar to me. Uh... yes. Now I understand. Treb Bor yit-NE explained. Yes.

Jefferson: Go pay me a visit. Yeah, I'd love to meet you?

Luhluprahkto: Uh... what?

Jefferson: Go pay me a visit there.

Luhluprahkto: Ohhhhh yes. Now I understand [Giggles] what you mean. Treb Bor yit-NE explained. Future and past... now I understand.

Jefferson: Yeah. Okay. Will you think about it?

Luhluprahkto: Yes, perhaps this is a good idea to try one day. If I am ever in the area, the Pleiades region, I will stop and give you a visit.

Jefferson: How did you get this invitation?

Luhluprahkto: I am not sure if they need to give me one. If I am ready to come there I am sure they are ready to have me, right?

Jefferson: Right. How did you get this invitation to talk to me?

Luhluprahkto: Oh, the invitation for this? As I explained, Treb Bor yit-NE is very close to me. We have been old friends and he asked for a race that is looking like humans, so I decided to grab on to this immediately and speak to you.

Jefferson: Oh I see, so there was not other people who wanted to talk to us. It was...

Luhluprahkto: Oh I am sure there are many here that would. But they are listening now.

Jefferson: Wow. Say hello to them.

Luhluprahkto: Uh... you have about one billion hands that wave back to you.

Jefferson: [Laughter] Wow. Okay. So now, I will give you the floor for us to share your message in the name of your people and then if you wish I will be more than happy to answer one of your most interesting questions for me. And should you have further questions I will let you ask from Treb, okay?

Luhluprahkto: Okay.

Jefferson: I will now sit back and enjoy your message. Thank you!

Luhluprahkto: Alright Thank you. Hello planet Earth! It is very great to meet up with you today. I want to talk to you about a couple of ideas that can help you pursue happiness. When you are going down a road and you feel resistance, you have to jump over this resistance by understanding what it is that is resisting you. When this resistance is made to you, you have to sit and examine: what it is that is getting in the way of this progress. It is always accompanied by feelings that are usually negative, ones that aren't very positive for you. And this is the sign. This is what says, this is what is going to block you from being able to do what you want.

So when you do this, you have to examine it, think about it, and move on. When you sit and dwell on this, then it becomes issues of manifesting more road obstacles. You have to understand your existence is very quick. You can be as quick as you wish to in your own existence by changing. It is understood that your ideas in your planet goes from one, to one, to one, back and forth: sad and happy and mad and glad. And you can do this very quick. Well, this is an example of how you should act throughout your whole existence. Your existence can be taken from a bad point to a happy point in a very quick way. So this is what you are capable to do if you set your mind to it and believe that you are capable of doing this. Jumping from the negative ideas to the positive idea very quickly is a great way to avoid these complications.

Understanding my reality is what I make it at any point that I make it and I can change it right now. This is the greatest way to do that. Living in happiness is very easy to do. You find what excites you and you follow with no discrimination. No complications of ideas of what is wrong and what is right. No complications of ideas as if this is my highest excitement or my lower excitement?, because you already know! You will be very happy when you do it. If you are not doing something that makes you happy, remember what it is that makes you happy and do that.

Following that excitement is the greatest way to go. You are able to explore different avenues of what is making you happy. And doing this is a very great way to keep yourself and the most up light and expression of energy that you have. So going from this to the next is very easy but if one makes you very happy, stay with this. You do not have to jump unless you want to. That is also the other point of making your own ways, understanding you have an option to make a new one or stay with one that makes you very happy.

If you are already this way, exploring the happiness can be very complex if you let it, but it can also be very easy. And most in your race, right now, is dealing with just this problem. Exact ideas of how to be happy. It is easy! All you have to do is be happy, know what makes you happy and do it.

Understanding ideas of economy, money, all these things... but understand that there are millions of people on your planet, right now, that are very, very happy and do not have one penny. It is because of the idea of humans tends to be, the only way you can be happy is by having money. When in fact, the only way to truly be happy is to have no money at all! Uh... not meaning that you are broken, but meaning that you don't have to use money. Uh... So, let me straighten this idea or you can run away with it. [Laughter]

Jefferson: [Giggles] Right.

Luhluprahkto: So, going through these ideas, is very well. And it is very easy to be happy. All you have to do is live in that love and excitement and be who you want to be, how you want to be it. And let nothing stand on your way by giving it any power. If you feel other people are doing this to you: "I could be happy if it wasn't for other people", they are only testing you to see what truly makes you happy. They are only a part of you anyway. So when you say, relationships that can make me happy... remove that from your brain, because you are not truly stopped by anyone else. Only the way that you let them react with you and you with them. And if you follow all of this ideas and jump to whatever makes you most happy, you'll always be happy. And this is what we hope to share with you.

Jefferson: Wow. That is excellent! Thank you very much.

Luhluprahkto: Yes. I hope that it was very great for you.

Jefferson: It was. By the way, how are you connecting right now to us? Are you sitting in a butterfly position having your hands closed and the eyes closed? How are you connecting to us?

Luhluprahkto: No. I am walking around doing a couple of things. I haven't perfected it quite as some has. On my planet some can do literally five, or six things at once with their mind and body; but I am able to walk and talk.

Jefferson: Fantastic. Okay. We are approaching the end of our communication. How did enjoy giving us the message, connecting to our energy... how did you enjoy it?

Luhluprahkto: I was very happy. It is the state that I prefer to be in. And giving it to you, hoping that even if one person can read this, hear this or do whatever they want to experience it, that it will make them half as happy as I am too now. And that will make my happiness even more happy.

Jefferson: Right, so let's make a wish that whenever someone reads this, a rainbow shows up in your planet.

Luhluprahkto: Alright. Let's apply this to the idea of connecting to everyone who connects to what I am saying now.

Jefferson: Yes! Lovely. Now, do you have any question... particular, most interesting, from you to me? Not that I am the representative of Earth, but perhaps you can have some idea of how I think by my answer.

Luhluprahkto: Instead of approaching it that way, that puts you as a representation as you said you are not, let me put you as an individual entity. What is the greatest thing that makes you excited?

Jefferson: It is to not only be able to realize without resistance that there is intelligent life outside of Earth, but to communicate with them and have this information to be useful for others who will come after me once they start realizing what I have realized a couple of years ago. That is it. I think that is what makes me most happy and is my highest excitement. Yeah.

Luhluprahkto: Oh thank you for sharing.

Jefferson: Great. So... yeah... what are your surroundings like, there, right now?

Luhluprahkto: Well, right now I am in the midst of the village that we live in. It is very bright. Very... many people that are dancing around... uh... maybe not physically the way you understand dancing but they are dancing inside. They are focused on the conversation right now and very happy to hear the information that you gave.

Jefferson: Fantastic. Okay. So, my thank you very much to all of you. May God bless your planet! [Giggles]

Luhluprahkto: Oh thank you. [Giggles] And as I said earlier. One billion people are telling good bye to you.

Jefferson: Fantastic, thank you very much. And whenever you wish, pay me a visit!

Luhluprahkto: I will try to pay you a visit in more than one area of your consciousness. How is this?

Jefferson: That is fantastic!

Luhluprahkto: Oh thank you for sharing it.

Jefferson: You have a great day!

Luhluprahkto: Alright and you do too.

Jefferson: Thank you!

Extraterrestrial Life

ZANETLY HUMANS

Chapter 3
08/23/2012

Planet: Zanetly
Lifespan: 2600 years

Spokesperson: Kroyzep
Age: 1245 years old

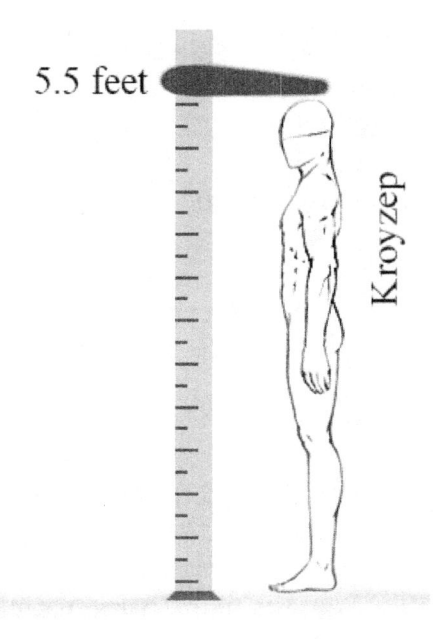

5.5 feet

Kroyzep

Future Human: Greetings Jefferson!

Jefferson: Greetings to you my friend. Who are you?

Future Human: My name is Kroyzep

Jefferson: Okay. And why is that? Why that is your name?

Kroyzep: It is the name that was given to me, by my race of people.

Jefferson Viscardi 53

Jefferson: So, it is not like your parents when you were born said: "oh this is what is going to be his name".

Kroyzep: No. It is similar to a designated name, like your planet has, but it is given from a group or a society instead of one or two individuals.

Jefferson: Right and what is your constellation? Where are you from?

Kroyzep: Uh... in your star systems... I am referring back to Treb. So if you give me one second.

***[Silence]

Kroyzep: It is close to Lyra. In between Lyra and Cygnus.

***[Cygnus is a northern constellation lying on the plane of the Milky Way. Its name is the Latinized Hellenic (Greek) word for swan. One of the most recognizable constellations of the northern summer and autumn, it features a prominent asterism known as the Northern Cross (in contrast to the Southern Cross). Cygnus was among the 48 constellations listed by the 2nd century astronomer Ptolemy, and it remains one of the 88 modern constellations. Source: Wikipedia].

Jefferson: Wow. Okay. Is there a name for your planet?

Kroyzep: Zanetly is the name of our people and also the name of the planet.

Jefferson: And is your solar system like ours?

Kroyzep: It is similar. With one star and many rotations but

Extraterrestrial Life

many of our planets, in the rotation are more oblong. They tend to get close to the star and then move out. Most of the inward system, planets are these way. The outward ones are more circular as most of yours are. And one that is on the inside, is the last in orbit of the inner planets. This one takes the representation and characteristics of the outward planets. It takes a circular motion around.

Jefferson: Okay. How many planets do you have in your solar system?

Kroyzep: Eleven.

Jefferson: And which one is your planet?

Kroyzep: The fifth. It is the furthest outside of the smaller planets than there is a large break, a large amount of space and once this happens, the sixth through eleventh are on the outer realms.

Jefferson: Oh I see. So what color is your planet when we look from outside?

Kroyzep: If you come above our planet and look down, it is brown.

Jefferson: Do you have oceans and spaces like that, like we have?

Kroyzep: No. It is mostly a consistency of dirt. No vegetation. It is only soil and rocks.

Jefferson: Do you find that interesting?

Kroyzep: Yes. It is a preference of our race. We are entering a new level of consciousness and once this is done we will experience more changes throughout the system. But right now this fits our people very well.

Jefferson: Understood. What then, density are you?

Kroyzep: In the time now we are moving from the fourth to the fifth density.

Jefferson: Are you excited?

Kroyzep: Yes. We are very happy to have growth. We are very happy to move in our conscious evolution or stepping ladder. The fourth and fifth is not proper in the ways that we see levels of evolution. In the evolution that we see there are twenty-seven steps. And this would be the fifteenth.

Jefferson: This would be the fifteenth level out of twenty-seven?

Kroyzep: Yes.

Jefferson: Wow. And what is the size of your planet? Is that as big as Earth?

Kroyzep: It is much bigger. It is maybe three or four times the size. I am not very sure of the exact size of your planet but from what I know of it, it would be three or four times.

Jefferson: Wow. And how many people do you have there?

Kroyzep: Seventeen, eighteen million.

Jefferson: Okay, well. Not a whole lot.

Kroyzep: No. Not compared to Earth which I understand has a very huge amounts in a smaller area.

Jefferson: Right. So what do you look like?

Kroyzep: I look much as your people do. We are about 5.5 feet tall. We are light tan or brown color. We have a very long hair, black hair, that comes to the back of our knees and we all have brown eyes and this is an average description of our people.

Jefferson: But do you also have green or blue eyed people?

Kroyzep: No. Brown is the only color. We have darker eyes than most races in our... that look like us because we have much brighter star. So the darkness is needed to filter some of that out.

Jefferson: Even in the fourth density?

Kroyzep: Oh yes. Light is still perceived but light that comes from the star is still made up of a different material than the light of your star. It is a much higher vibration of light. And our eyes are still used as an organ to experience visually.

Jefferson: And if you were to walk amongst us on Earth, would we realize you are form another planet?

Kroyzep: Perhaps with the shape of our chins? And ears? It would look very odd to you. But for the most part, I don't think it would be recognizable.

Jefferson: So you have pointy ears?

Kroyzep: No... They are elongated.

Jefferson: But upwards, downwards, just to the side?

Kroyzep: Downwards.

Jefferson: Oh down? Ah, like dogs!

Kroyzep: [Discreet Giggle] Yes.

Jefferson: Wow, that is cool. So your ears are nothing like ours.

Kroyzep: No. It is not exactly like dogs. The bottom part of the ears that are longer. The lobe.

Jefferson: Oh okay. Wow. How long do you sustain life in your physical body?

Kroyzep: 2500, 2600; that is an average.

Jefferson: And how old are you?

Kroyzep: Me, personally, is 1245.

Jefferson: Okay. So you are half way there. How long does it take for your planet to go around the Sun, once: one day?

Kroyzep: About one and a half time as yours. Thirty six.

Jefferson: While we are talking about your planet, could you tell me if you guys have governments?

Kroyzep: Oh no. There are only structures of groups that work together for various achievement. Even though we are all connected, the various achievements are all done by individual groups and then each individual group works together with the other groups for achievement of different things. Scientific and technology means, cultural means. Various items. Clothing. Things that you would need, on a daily basis. And all of the groups work together as one large group. I am not sure what type of society you would label this?

Jefferson: So how do you know that you are not using too much of the capacity of resources of your planet? Do you have computers, or... technology?

Kroyzep: Oh yes, we have technology. The resources of our planet are very abundant and we are using what we need. The way our planet is rich in resources, is not the same as yours. To humans you see water, food, trees... all of those types of resources. And for us its metal. Metal is what we use for everything.

Jefferson: I see. So are your cities close in appearance to ours at all?

Kroyzep: They are very large cities but not the same size as yours. The greater cities on your planet makes ours look very small. But for the size of our race the cities are fairly big.

Jefferson: But do you have building and undergrounds, trains, cars...

Kroyzep: The buildings that we have are above and underground. If I am comparing it to something that you would recognize, maybe three or four floors below and a few of them are above, perhaps eight. That would be a representation of the buildings. They are very structured, very squarely. So perhaps some of the skyscrapers that you have would be a great representation. Vehicles that we use... there are many types. But the main resources of transportation is the ability to jump from one side to the next, in the air.

Jefferson: Wow. So you have strong legs.

Kroyzep: The technology is what brings us. A ship of sorts.

Jefferson: Oh okay. But do you mean jumping as bending time and space or jump the way we would jump rope.

Kroyzep: From landing at one point, moving to the next in a looping way or an arch way. That is a transport. It is very quick. Our propulsion systems take us very quick, very far. We are able to shift our own selves in the physical body to various places. But this is not needed. Our technology can move there in sufficient enough time.

Jefferson: How do you work out the education in your planet?

Kroyzep: For education systems, each one is taught from the elder in their family. And once they are done learning all the things that they wish to know then they will go out to the rest of the community to learn a very specific thing. They join the groups in a workforce environment and once they are done working they find if they enjoyed it enough to stay. If they don't they move to the next group of workforce and join it, or move to the next.

Jefferson: Are you in the future?

Kroyzep: Slightly.

Jefferson: How many years?

Kroyzep: Maybe five thousand.

Jefferson: Slightly?! Okay. Five thousand years in the future. Hmm. That is a lot. How... how do you see God?

Kroyzep: God is an imaginary figure. It is something that people give a designation to him. So that they can understand the creation affect, the system of creation. If you see God as a creator. It is a creation of energy and this energy brings forth growth of consciousness and consciousness grows into an environment that we think of to be of physical nature.

Jefferson: How do you relate to music?

Kroyzep: Uh... music... Oh... the sound being played... we have no specific music.

Jefferson: Okay. Do you travel outside your solar system?

Kroyzep: Oh yes. Very often.

Jefferson: Okay. What is your job in your race?

Kroyzep: For me is a transportation specialist. Which means I have a great understanding of the technology that we use to transport.

Jefferson: Oh. Do you wear clothing?

Kroyzep: Oh yes. We wear clothes.

Jefferson: Do they look like ours? Or...

Kroyzep: Uh... no. It is rounded. Almost appearing to be a bubble. That goes from the neck to the ankles.

Jefferson: It would be really fun in our race!

Kroyzep: Yes. I think it wouldn't be anything similar to what you are used to.

Jefferson: And I think that our clothing would be pretty fun for you in your race right? To look at. It would be strange.

Kroyzep: Very colorful.

Jefferson: Right. And for you guys they are not that colorful? No?

Kroyzep: The darker colors are preferred by us. This shows in the manifestations of, not only our planet but our appearance.

Jefferson: So you guys are not dark. You have also white people... in the sense of skin... whitish...

Kroyzep: Oh no. It is all similar, to the same color.

Jefferson: Brown.

Kroyzep: Yes. Brown or tanned.

Jefferson: Okay. And how are you guys born?

Kroyzep: We are born through a sexual nature.

Jefferson: Right. So it is the same as us. You are created through the union of the sperm and the egg. And do you stay in the mom's womb until you are born?

Kroyzep: The way we understand it... you are not here until you are born. The growth in the womb of the females is not truly us.

Jefferson: Right. So how long does it take for you to be born?

Kroyzep: Probably around thirty two or thirty three...

Jefferson: Days?

Kroyzep: Years of your time.

Jefferson: No. No. No, for you to actually be born from the time that you are conceived.

Kroyzep: Yes. About thirty three years.

Jefferson: So your mom has carried you in her womb for all those years?

Kroyzep: Yes. Cycles of reproductions... the energies are appropriate. Every thirty two or thirty three. In between that time of your markers of years to procreate.

Jefferson: Oh so every cycle you procreate meaning you don't have sexual relationship in between.

Kroyzep: Oh... no. We do have sexual relations very often. But those are the times... the children come.

Jefferson: Are men and women the same? Do they look the

same? Do they have the same hair color, and eye color?

Kroyzep: Yes. They have the similar appearances.

Jefferson: Right. But women have boobs!

Kroyzep: Not any difference in the chest areas, like yours do. There is difference in the heights of legs.

Jeffeson: Okay. How did you receive this invitation?

Kroyzep: Uh... there was an energy that I felt coming. Many of us felt it. Few of the ones who are in our race whose job is to seek out other races spoke to this entity that connects us. And he asked if there was anyone willing to speak to you.

Jefferson: So how did this come to you? Did they say: "Hey..." What is your name again?

Kroyzep: My name is Kroy-zep!

Jefferson: Did they say "hey Kroyzep, there is this guy and do you want to..." How... how did they get to you?

Kroyzep: As a part of my responsibility of being one who has a transportation expert... because I do this job I am responsible for all off world ventures: to prepare the machines, to have them leave. And because all of the ones who go to meet other entities come through this area to get into the craft and to leave, this is an associated responsibility.

Jefferson: Wow. So you are also an ambassador for your planet?

Kroyzep: Uh... I suppose that you can see it that way?

Jefferson: So what do you know about Earth?

Kroyzep: I know somethings from some of the ones who have traveled outside. When they come back they come to my area so I am the first to absorb the ideas and energies of what they have seen from your race or understood. So I have a general understanding.

Jefferson: So what is the thing that you most like about Earth?

Kroyzep: The environment in the deserts that you have, seem to be very refreshing and very nice. It is much lighter than our planet and this can be appealing to the eye, sometimes. Sometimes the water that you have around... it is different from ours. So it is not that I would wish to go into the water or be around it. But to see it is a very beautiful thing.

Jefferson: And what is the thing you like the least?

Kroyzep: I don't have a thing I like the least. There are things I prefer less.

Jefferson: Which is the thing you prefer the least?

Kroyzep: My preferences of not wishing to do things or wishing to be in other groups of workforce. To not extend relationships to entities that have tried to manipulates races of ours in the past or races that are close to us in connection. Those would be the least.

Jefferson: Okay. I will leave you now. Give you a couple of minutes... actually as long as you need, to go ahead and share with us your message. Go ahead.

Kroyzep: The message that I wish to express is that you are not alone in your area. Humans tend to see the idea of being the only ones. Even though this has become more understood by your race moral people are starting to see the validity of all things that are more of understanding of where we come from.

We reach out to many races, we speak to many races and we connect non-physically to other races. And even through this, we have a very small idea of how much life there is. Feeling insignificant is not the way to approach this.

The feeling of insignificance that some humans who do understand the amount of life there is the opposite way to go on the mindset that can keep you healthy, which is to become excited by this. To understand that anything that is different from you, is not bad if it appears to be plain, ordinary. This is not a bad thing! If it appears to be so different you cannot understand it... this is not a bad thing! Opening up the ability to love is one thing that Treb Bor yit-NE would tell you, but I would tell you to open your minds. To understand the greatness of everything that is. And thank you for connecting to our race.

Jefferson: Thank you very much! So did you enjoy this idea of connecting to us and sharing your message?

Kroyzep: Yes. I always enjoy the responsibilities that I have and this is why I do that.

Jefferson: How are you connecting to me? I know it is through Treb. But, how are you doing it? Are you sitting down, closing your eyes in meditation stances?

Kroyzep: There is a dark room that we use for long distance broadcasting when we connect to other races. Especially those who are outside of our density. We use the room. It is completely void of life and it is completely silent. This helps us focus our energy into the machine that is in the chair and helps us broadcast further.

Jefferson: Okay. So, is there any question you have I could share a point of view on about with you, as a human from Earth?

Kroyzep: Uh… if there is anything that you want to say to me I will accept it as a comment. But I have no inquires specifically.

Jefferson: Fantastic! What I want to say to you is… actually… thank you very much it is very kind of you taking the time out of your duties and your day to share with us your message. I appreciate that and I thank you very much for that.

Kroyzep: I thank you for taking your time and your responsibilities to speak to me as well. In my understanding that is your love for reaching out and helping others to understand such connections.

Jefferson: Indeed. So, thank you very much. Have yourself a wonderful time in your lovely planet!

Kroyzep: Thank you and you have a very happy time with yours as well.

$OLDRANTEE HUMAN$

Chapter 4
08/23/2012

Message from Soldrantee
Lifespan: 1000 years

Spokesperson:
Prontlasfornoplarecskitpla
Age: 771 years old

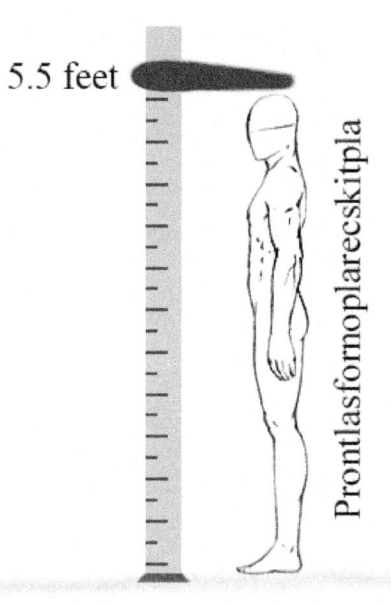

5.5 feet

Future Human: How are you doing Jefferson?

Jefferson: Hey who are you?

Future Human: My name is Pront açsjf açi!&#$%¨% Kitla.

Jefferson: Wow. Can you repeat that?

Future Human: Prontlasforknotlasrechkitla.

Jefferson: Uh... Okay. Beautiful! Short and sweet! Where are you from? Are you a boy or a girl?

Prontlasforknotlasrechkitla: I am a male.

Jefferson: Okay. And... Uh... Where are you from?

***[We will shorten the name as a way of transforming it into a symbol for editing purposes, but know that his name continues to be: Prontlasforknotlasrechkitla]

Pron...kitla: Uh... where am I from?...

Jefferson: Yes. What constellation are you from?

Pron...kitla: Oh. The area that is known to your people by the little kite. One moment I will see with Treb.

***[Silence]

Pron...kitla: I don't think he knows the name either. It is the one that looks like a kite. [Delphinus]

Jefferson: Okay. And what is the name of your planet?

Pron...kitla: Soldrantee.

Jefferson: What is the size of your planet? Is it as big as ours?

Pron...kitla: It is similar in size.

Jefferson: How long is a day for you?

Pron...kitla: Maybe a couple of weeks in your time. Two.

Jefferson: And do you guys have in your planet what we call hurricane, earthquakes...

Pron...kitla: Oh no. We have a very calm environment.

Jefferson: What is the color of your skies?

Pron...kitla: When you are looking up or when you are looking down?

Jefferson: When you are looking up from the ground.

Pron...kitla: When you are looking up it is an orange but when you are looking down, it is blue.

Jefferson: Wow. How many people do you have in your planet?

Pron...kitla: About five hundred and fifty million.

Jefferson: And is your solar system like ours, or different?

Pron...kitla: No. It is very different. With your solar system, to my understanding you have one star and eight planets. Is that correct?

Jefferson: Yeah, about it.

Pron...kitla: Yes and ours we have three stars and we have thirty nine planets.

Jefferson: Three stars, thirty nine planets! Wow. Which planet are you from?

Pron...kitla: Twenty first!

Jefferson: And how many stars are there around your planet?

Pron...kitla: All of the planets come around. All three of them.

Jefferson: So how is it placed? Like, you have three stars in the middle and they go around these three stars like that?

Pron...kitla: Yes. That way. They go around all three of them.

Jefferson: Right. That was simple, right?

Pron...kitla: Oh yes.

Jefferson: What density are you?

Pron...kitla: We are from the fourth density.

Jefferson: You seem to be a very happy person.

Pron...kitla: Yes. Being able to talk to you is very exciting.

Jefferson: How are people in your society born?

Pron...kitla: When we are very small like the size of a really small... what is small on your planet?

Jefferson: a Guinea pig is pretty small! Hamsters are smaller though!

Pron...kitla: Uh... I am not sure... oh no. A Guinea pig is bigger. It is the size of a bottle cap.

Jefferson: Oh.

Pron...kitla: When we are about that size, we are placed into an environment that is void of all liquid, sound and light. Like a vacuum but there is air that goes through. Oxygen, nitrogen, those types of molecules.

Jefferson: So... but you are conceived the same way we are. From a lovely sexual relationship.

Pron...kitla: Oh no. [Giggles] No. No. When we are made... uh... from the people who are scientific... scientists that go into a laboratory and they take genetics that are basic from our race. Like an archive of genes and then they put together at once so that the bodies are very similar.

Jefferson: So the women don't fabricate eggs and the men don't fabricate sperms?

Pron...kitla: Oh no. That phased out. Our race... even though it is not egg and sperm, as exactly as your people, it is similar in the way that we used to do a long time ago. In the early third density and even into the middle and late of the third density. And once we moved to forth we come outside of these ideas of sexual relationship and we are able to do it scientifically.

Jefferson: Do you still have sexual organs?

Pron...kitla: Yes and we tend to have relations with others too.

Jefferson: ...sexual relations.

Pron...kitla: Oh yes. This is a great enjoyment for our society. I do not think that anyone on our planet would give this away.

Jefferson: Do you go to the toilet like we do to pee and for number 2?

Pron...kitla: Oh, no. [Giggle] The excretion... [giggles] process that your people tend to use has been gone for a while.

Jefferson: Oh so when you drink something it gets our through sweat?

Pron...kitla: Uh... no. Everything is being used. Our systems don't produce waist.

Jefferson: Right and you don't eat more than you need.

Pron...kitla: Oh no. Yes. We all have a small amount in portions that we all eat.

Jefferson: I love you name you know? I just love it. I wish I could pronounce it. I don't know how the channeler can pronounce it. Really. Can you say it again?

Pron...kitla: Yes! It is... do you want me to make it easier for you to understand it and break it up into small parts? Prontlasforknotlasrechkitla:

Jefferson: Yes. Perhaps!

Pron...kitla: Pront... like pront. Las... Fornop... La... Recs... Kitpla.

Jefferson: Kitpla?

Pron...kitla: Yes.

Jefferson: Okay.

*** [So far we were under the impression he said:

Prontlasforknotlasrechkitla but after saying bit by bit we realized he said: Prontlasfornoplarecskitpla. For abreviation we will use thus then Pront[...]kitpla].

Jefferson: So, what do you look like? Oh wait! I will... I will call you just Kitpla!

Pront[...]kitpla: [Giggles] You can do this.

Jefferson: Thank you. [Laughter]

Kitpla: [Giggles] That is better for you to do.

Jefferson: [Laughter]

Kitpla: We are about 9 feet tall. And we are very skinny. Slim. Slimmer than the slimmer types of humans.

Jefferson: Wow.

Kitpla: But our facial structure looks very similar to yours. Only adjusted into a smaller area.

Jefferson: Wow. So do you think if you were to walk amongst us you would realize you are not from here?

Kitpla: [Giggles] I would hope that the human perception could catch this.

Jefferson: [Laughter]. So it is not just the ears or the chin. It is much more, right?

Kitpla: Oh yes.

Jefferson: But the way the things sit on your face is the same right? You look like a human, in that sense.

Kitpla: Oh yes. Yes. A very tall thin one, but yes. We have the very similar looks to yours.

Jefferson: Okay. And what is the color of your eyes?

Kitpla: It is a pinkish color!

Jefferson: But pinkish is girly.

Kitpla: [Giggles] Is this what your race believe?

Jefferson: Yes.

Kitpla: Oh. Pink is a very great color. It is one that is very strong in energy.

Jefferson: Oh okay. Is that the women have the same color as man?

Kitpla: Oh yes.

Jefferson: And for your skin? What color is that?

Kitpla: It is very white.

Jefferson: Oh okay. And the hair is... for male and female is it the same?

Kitpla: It is a little different. With a man it is much wider and longer and the women is more compressed and shorter.

Jefferson: Oh. You know it sounds really strange in my mind when you say compressed. [Laughter]

Kitpla: [Giggles] Why? Why it is that? Does it mean anything?

Jefferson: Yeah, compressed… it is like when you get an orange and you squeeze it.

Kitpla: Oh squeeze. Yes.

Jefferson: You mean… but you mean short, right?

Kitpla: Short and not as wide. The hair tends to be very fluffy!

Jefferson: Wow. Fluffy like the fur of cats?

Kitpla: Kind of like that. Yes. The big cats that you have.

Jefferson: Oh Tiger.

Kitpla: The other big one. Lion! They are kind of fluffy like that. Yeah.

Jefferson: Do you wear clothing?

Kitpla: We wear clothing over our leg areas…

Jefferson: But to hide your… your thing?

Kitpla: [Giggles] No. It is just to have a style that we all appreciate. There is no need… [Giggles] to cover the genital region if we don't want to. There is nothing embarrassing about it. I understand your race is still in the giggle mode in what concerns this idea of genitals…

Jefferson: Right. And for curves!

Kitpla: Yes.

Jefferson: Right. So you guys don't have much curve right? Because you are plain flat.

Kitpla: [Laughter] Yeah. Yes.

Jefferson: How long can you inhabit your body?

Kitpla: For about 1000 years.

Jefferson: And how old are you?

Kitpla: I am about 771.

Jefferson: Oh. So you are like... middle age. Nah... you have already passed the mark of the middle age sir.

Kitpla: Yes.

Jefferson: Do you have governments?

Kitpla: We have what you say to be representatives of our different areas. We have major cities that are around the whole planet. There are 12 that are huge and there are other smaller ones. And each town has a representative of the ideas and enjoyment of the other. And they get together. And they help to give us ideas that better ourselves as a complete race. But there is no ruling factor. It is more of ideas about how we can do things in a better way to improve ourselves through our whole lives, through our existences that are over and over as a race completely. Not only for our lives, but for the lives of the next generations and the ones after that. Just to improve our race completely.

Jefferson: Wow. Do you live anywhere close to Pleenaki? [Jefferson's human future self located at the Pleiades in a planet called Plenatalaka, 2000 years in the future.].

Kitpla: Uh... No. That is... uh... about 1000 light years.

Jefferson: Are your cities the same as ours?

Kitpla: No. Not the way your cities are... very boxy and tall and small, a mixture of all things... Our cities are round. The way that the cities look from above is round and all of the buildings are round too.

Jefferson: How do you guys process education?

Kitpla: I am not sure what you mean.

Jefferson: How... because... for instance: when we are small we go to the kinder garden and then we go through the schooling process throughout the years as a child, to get prepared for our life... we do that to lean stuff. So how does it work, the process of education in your planet?

Kitpla: There is no true process. Life is its own teachings and uh... sometimes even failure teaches you. Life is a process. It is the greatest teacher that we have. Uh... There is no specific ideas of learning or education. We just exist.

Jefferson: Right but don't they have universities? Like... where you go to learn how to operate a physical body. How to implant hair and eyes and hearts...

Kitpla: No. We do what we love on a daily basis and the things that we learn we apply for the benefit of the rest of our race.

Jefferson: Oh I see. So if someone wants to learn something you know, they don't go to classes, they come and talk to you.

Kitpla: They talk to their selves. They give theirselves the lesson. Through trial and error. And even the trial and error idea that your race uses is not really using of a trial and error. It is a trial and understanding of ways to get better. And this is how it is done. For you people, if you do something at your job and then you mess it up... sometimes you get frustrated, sometimes you get angry and it misplaces your mind. But for us it is a doing something that if it doesn't work out the exact way we wish it to, we continue to build from that. And this teaches ourself everything we need to know.

Jefferson: Okay. Do you guys have a system of transportation?

Kitpla: For our planet, we don't use transportation. We are able to connect our consciousnesses by an instant mean. But when we leave the planet we do have parts of the city that are inhabitted in that are lifted up and leave the planet.

Jefferson: Right. And the people that don't want to go, they stay homeless.

Kitpla: [Laughter] No. It is their house that they take.

Jefferson: Oh I see. So if you want to come and visit me you bring your entire home.

Kitpla: Oh yes. That is... the cities are built from that. But if we leave it is for a reason so there is no reason to keep your dwelling there if you are leaving.

Jefferson: [Laughter]

Kitpla: Right?

Jefferson: I know. I know. We will start doing the same thing in the future. Hopefully! Uh... by the way. Are you in the future?

Kitpla: Uh... yes.

Jefferson: How far?

Kitpla: Uh... let me... let me... connect to Treb to see if this... uh... is allowable to speak about? Uh... because... well... one second.

Jefferson: Okay.

***[Silence]

Kitpla: Uh... okay. About 700 years.

Jefferson: Why were you worried? That is just numbers! [Laughter]

Kitpla: Oh I know. [Giggles] But with idea that you are still a planet that is removed from contact, it was something that I wanted to make sure that wouldn't affect you.

Jefferson: That makes of you a very kind person.

Kitpla: [Giggles] Thank you for that.

Jefferson: What is your job in your race?

Kitpla: There is really not a job. We do what we want. What I love the most is the ability to connect outside of this planet. Mentally and sometimes physically too.

Jefferson: So you definitely have already traveled to other planets with your house.

Kitpla: Oh yes. Very often.

Jefferson: So you bring everything! You certainly don't have bathrooms, right? Because you don't uh... need them. So what does your house look like?

Kitpla: It is round around the edges and a very long elongated arch on the top and a less elongated on the bottom.

Jefferson: Okay. That is it?

Kitpla: Uh...

Jefferson: Do you have windows?

Kitpla: No. There is no need to see outside. We know it is there.

Jefferson: Okay. Do you have beauty in your planet, like oceans and trees and...

Kitpla: There is environment that is rich in life. Water areas, tree areas... It has a little bit of both of these but it is spread out fairly well.

Jefferson: Do you pray?

Kitpla: Prayer? Uh... I suppose it depends on the definition of what prayer is.

Jefferson: I will teach you children's prayer. You put your two hands together and say: Dear Jesus please protect me and my family. That is it!

Kitpla: And that is what a prayer is?

Jefferson: Yes.

Kitpla: Oh no. We don't need a protection from Jesus. I don't think that anyone from that name would hurt us.

Jefferson: [Giggles] No! He is the one who is the protector.

Kitpla: Oh. I didn't know.

Jefferson: He is the one that is going to protect you from the disembodied annoying lost guys.

Kitpla: Oh no. We've disconnected from our... Our disconnection was long ago. There is no need to protect us from it. We have already removed ourselves from that.

Jefferson: Wow. Congratulations to you! So. You don't have religion then.

Kitpla: No religion as the idea of what most tend to think religion is. We have an idea of values, an idea of what we believe to be right. And we also have a belief... for other people to do as they wish and if you call morals, religion... then I suppose. But that is not the definition that you give. Then no.

Jefferson: How do you see God?

Kitpla: We have an energy that surrounds us. For our planet, this could be considered God from how you see it. But for our race, every planet has its own energy. And each energy is very special. But there is one energy that makes all of the energies and this energy is similar from the idea of God, a Creator of sorts.

Jefferson: Do you speak to angels? To spirit guides? Or stuff like that?

Kitpla: We speak to many different things. Spirit guide... one who guides us in spirit? We talk to relatives that are in between the cycles. We talk to many people. For guidance perhaps not, for better ideas... yes.

Jefferson: How do you relate to music?

Kitpla: Music is something of a pure vibration. That is what music is. It is a sound, a vibrational sound. And this is used in our everyday life. For everything. Vibration is very important. Each individual vibration is given its own meaning and its own energy. And each one is used for different things. It is very important to have music. Because the energies that make every planet are a song within itself. You just have to be able to open your energy enough to hear it. Music is what dictates your soul. It is what makes everything that is important to us to be as real as it is, in a multidimensional way.

Jefferson: Wow. And still in that idea of music, do you have pets? [Laughter]

Kitpla: [Giggles] And this has to do with music you said?

Jefferson: Yes. Because the pets make sounds, right?

Kitpla: Uh... I suppose that a pet would, but for us the life that is carried on our planet is only more simple lives. Trees or plants or smaller.

Jefferson: Oh man. You have to hear some birds we have here. They sing so beautifully.

Kitpla: Oh yes. I have an understanding of the sound now. And that is something I truly wish to experience more intimately.

Jefferson: Right. So why don't you come over and pay me a dinner or something?

Kitpla: I am not sure you would eat our food very well.

Jefferson: No, but you can come over and I can take you down here to the local restaurant and then I can pay you a dinner.

Kitpla: If the rest of your race agrees, then I will come for a dinner. [Giggles] But until then I am afraid that that won't be something within my ability to do for worry of affecting you.

Jefferson: Wow. Would you affect me in any sense if we were to meet one on one?

Kitpla: Yes. The energy in itself of a higher consciousness is one that can affect lower consciousnesses. Uh...

Jefferson: Whoa that would just make me wiser!

Kitpla: Yes! And that is the effect that it can have but sometimes the effect can be the opposite. It depends on a specific vibration that is how this plays out.

Jefferson: Nahhh. I can't get dumber than this! [Laughter]

Kitpla: [Giggles] I am sure you are not giving yourself enough credit.

Jefferson: Nah I was just kidding. But what was the side effect that can happen? Like having a psychotic shock?

Kitpla: Sometimes. Physical illnesses. Depending on how we approach.

Jefferson: Right.

Kitpla: Depending on whether we approach entities in our own density or level... then it becomes much more hard of energy or a larger energy... and even though they can't see it or experience it with their senses, their soul cannot feel the effect and this can make the physical body ill.

Jefferson: You are pretty savvy on those ideas, huh?

Kitpla: This is the reason why I have a great understanding of not wanting to affect other races for that reason. I have understood ideas that I have seen from others or heard and experienced connectivity from ones who did not have the same beliefs that we do. Ones who didn't mind to come down and visit races who weren't quite ready yet.

Jefferson: So you have heard already of a side effect that did happen to a human being that received another human from another planet, who was not ready yet, and went into a kind of psychotic shock and had to be taken to the hospital.

Kitpla: Not for your race specifically, but for other races who were a little earlier in the evolution line.

Jefferson: Wow. Okay. So, how did you get this invitation?

Kitpla: For me it is a natural walk to experience outside consciousnesses that are not from our planet. And I connect out to all feelings of incoming...

Jefferson: calls.

Kitpla: ...connections. Or... yes. Calls, or connections. And I received this and my joy was the highest to do it. So I wanted to speak as soon as I could. The time that I first understood this was... uh... maybe if you look at the time linearly, uh... yesterday in your time.

Jefferson: Wow. And what do you know about Earth?

Kitpla: I know many things of Earth, I understand the ideas of perceptions and mindsets of some. Not all. It is very hard to reach out to a race that has as many different consciousnesses on one place at one time, to understand all of them. But the collective consciousness has a good idea of what is going on below and we understand this. We understand physical attributes. The dimensional attributes. There is much that we do understand.

Jefferson: Wow. Do you like any animals in particular that we have?

Kitpla: That is one aspect that we have not looked into greatly. It is the consciousness of a human that is interesting to us. Because if we interact with these other entities, the second density, the first denstity... then we are okay to interact with them. Their consciousness is not large enough to pick us up in a way that can disturb them. And this is not said offensively or meanly but an average human's energy tends to be slightly imbalanced. And imbalanced energy that affects negatives. Most of the second and first density animals from your planet tend to be very aligned, very well with their planet and dwelling.

Jefferson: Right. Right. Yeah. That doesn't offend. You can go ahead! [Giggles] Yeah, we know. We are kind of... a little behind. Well then... great. So, I understand you have a message for us. This is the time for us... that we have been waiting for to hear your message. So feel free; take your time and I will sit back and listen to you.

Kitpla: Greetings Earth. This is Prontlasfornoplarecskitpla and I want to say hello from the Soldrantee. We wish to welcome you in the great exchange of love and information and we start out by expressing ideas of connecting to each other, connecting to your own selves with an understanding of who you are. This in change will give you better connections to the ones around you. Before you are able to move outside of your own planet to greet others in the way that we wish to greet you, you must be able to greet each other.

    We are not judging you when we say that wars and the hunger and the financial systems are faulted. We only need to express this to you to show you that there are better ways. You cannot even start fathoming the possibilities of how great your race truly is until you can see this strength within yourself. To look inside of yourself and to see that you are worth being a great person and a soul. You are worth connecting to others and teaching them what you know and learning from them what they know; to be able to connect with each other and to love on a great grand scale, one that tends to make the greatest scale of your measurements useless. This type of love will unite, not only a race of people, but also many races to come to your people. I know that there is great excitement about the idea of speaking to other entities, of disclosure, of who is out there and what is going on. But before you are ready for the understanding of the larger ideas, you must understand how ready you are for this. You must understand that at your maximum capability, you are ready for much more than small ideas. That you are ready to create your own worlds, to create your own environments by thought alone. You are an energy of a race that is very strong. And once you know this, you will be able to manifest the greatness that you feel inside but can't yet get to the outside. Understanding this is the first part and in moving forward. And with this our people wish to give you great love and all the respect from us to you.

Jefferson: Wow. That was a beautiful message!

Kitpla: Thank you.

Jefferson: Did you enjoy sharing your message with us?

Kitpla: Oh yes. It was very great, exciting and I hope it is able to help anyone who reads it.

Jefferson: Now. How are you connecting to us? I know it is through Treb. But, are you... how are you doing it?

Kitpla: By what means?

Jefferson: Yes. Do you have an umbrella you are holding or... you know something to pick up energies from far away... or stuff like that?

Kitpla: Oh no. It is telepathically. Your race understands the telepathic idea of sending a thought signal?

Jefferson: Yes.

Kitpla: Yes. This is how we communicate.

Jefferson: But do you need to sit down? Do you have any assistance from other energies?

Kitpla: No. It is just a simple thought being sent. And a thought being received. An exchange of thought. And also slight interchanging of energy.

Jefferson: So it would look like I am talking to myself to an external observer.

Kitpla: Yes. Yes.

Jefferson: But when you send your thought, you don't move your mouth.

Kitpla: There is no need to move the mouth because it is a thought but yes, if they could hear the conversation they would believe you are speaking to yourself.

Jefferson: And there in your planet people can hear your thoughts, right?

Kitpla: Oh yes. And in your race some can but not all of them.

Jefferson: Right. Because you don't have anything to hide.

Kitpla: Oh yes. Sharing what you are to others is the greatest gift that you can give them. And when you do this then they are able to appreciate you for who you are and vice-versa.

Jefferson: That is a nice word. Did you like it? Vice-versa?

Kitpla: Yes. I understand that the man who sits here uses this word, sometimes.

Jefferson: Can you share a word from your language? It seems to be a very interesting language. How do you say in your language: much love with you or I love you, for instance?

Kitpla: The translation would be... uh.. Kolonateprito.

Jefferson: And what does that mean?

Kitpla: Love from me to you.

Jefferson: Kolonateprito.

Kitpla: Kolanataprito.

Jefferson: Kolanataprito.

Kitpla: Yes.

Jefferson: Wow. Okay. So, thank you very much. I have enjoyed this interaction, immensely.

Kitpla: It is a great pleasure for me as well.

Jefferson: Am I the first human being you talk to?

Kitpla: In this manner, yes.

Jefferson: Wow. I am very excited about that. I am part of your history now.

Kitpla: [Giggles] Yes. You are very much a part of it.

Jefferson: You write down okay. In a little note book: Jefferson Viscardi, it was the 28th of august, on Earth. It was a Tuesday. And a quarter to midnight!

Kitpla: I will so within. Within a small period of consciousness and let all know directly so they won't have to keep a record. But they will always have it in their hearts.

Jefferson: Anyways, in 13 years time you are always welcome to come and visit me okay?

Kitpla: Thank you.

Jefferson: Have yourself a lovely time. Until then, good bye.

Kitpla: Alright.

TRANKA HUMANS

Chapter 5
09/05/2012

Planet: [unpronounceable]
Lifespan: 700 years

Spokesperson: Haldra
Age: 375 years old

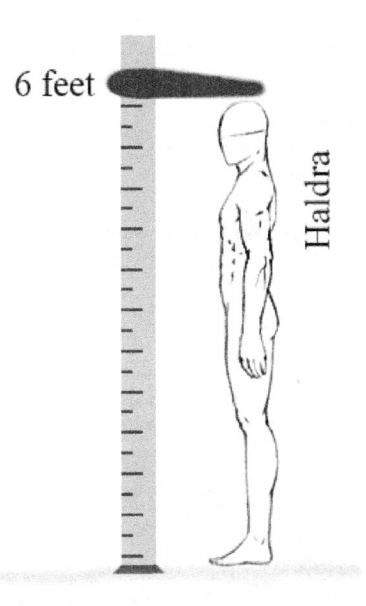

6 feet — Haldra

Galactic Human: Greetings!

Jefferson: Greetings to you. My name is Jefferson. I am from planet Earth and... who are you?

Galactic Human: My name is Haldra

Jefferson: Haldra... hmm... are you of a male or female orientation?

Haldra: I am a male.

Jefferson: What is your constellation?

Haldra: I have to extend myself to Treb. I am not aware of the skies settings in your planet...

Jefferson: Okay.

***[Silence]

Haldra: Uh... it is within the bull... uh... the Taurus bull.

Jefferson: Oh. I see. And what is the name of your planet?

Haldra: We don't have a specific designation name for it but our race is called the Tranka.

Jefferson: Tranka?

Haldra: Yes.

Jefferson: Alright. And what is the size of your planet? Is it as big as ours?

Haldra: It is close to the same size. I am not sure how much larger, or bigger. But it is very comparable to this.

Jefferson: But it is bigger.

Haldra: It is comparative. I am not sure of the exact size.

Jefferson: Wow. How long is a day for you?

Haldra: For us a day... uh... if I am counting in your time... seen in hours, and days, and the weeks... uh... one week and maybe three days.

Jefferson: What is the color of your skies?

Haldra: When we are looking at the sky we see a very dark purple.

Jefferson: And when you are coming from outside what color is the planet?

Haldra: The planet itself, coming from above it is red and orange and green.

Jefferson: Wow. And how many people do you have there?

Haldra: We have about 189 or 190 of the millions.

Jefferson: Right. Do you have hurricane... earthquakes?

Haldra: No. The unstable weather is very odd. Perhaps not for the type of being, in the level of consciousness that lives there. But for us it is not that way.

Jefferson: What density are you?

Haldra: We are in the fourth density. This is a level of density that you would see it as.

Jefferson: Right. Is your solar system like ours?

Haldra: In what ways do you mean?

Jefferson: Like we have only one star and nine planets... about that...

Haldra: It is similar to this. It has one star and thirteen planets.

Jefferson: I see. And which one is your planet?

Haldra: The fifth

Jefferson: And how many moons?

Haldra: Three moons.

Jefferson: Three moons? Wow. And whoa… what are the colors of the moons?

Haldra: When you are looking at a night sky, there is a shade of light purple to all of them but one glows a white with purple glowing; the other one is a gray with a purple glowing and the other one is orange and red with purple glowing.

Jefferson: How are the people in your planet born?

Haldra: They are born through a system. They are not truly born in the way that you think to be born. But we have many implants of the body… uh… of physical structure, that appear similar to all of us and these are genetically made and consciousness comes directly into them. The idea that you would have would be a clone. A genetic reproduction of similar being and consciousness is brought into them when they are ready to come into the cycle.

Jefferson: Understood. So you don't have sexual relations amongst you.

Haldra: No. We are only one gender.

Jefferson: Which is male...

Haldra: Yes.

Jefferson: Oh you are all male?

Haldra: Yes.

Jefferson: [Giggles] That is new. Why is that?

Haldra: Because of the way that we have made our system. Our parent race looks much like us but they were males and females. After their loss of life or connecting to another density when they are outside of our experience then we were left only to do with what we could. And there were only males that were there... all looking similar, all having the very same make up. Uh... in order to do this we were taught by them how to make bodies and when we do this then we reproduce the bodies and consciousness comes into the next body when the other life cycle is over.

Jefferson: So you look like twins.

Haldra: Very, very close in appearance. It would be hard for most to tell, unless they were from our race.

Jefferson: So this is my next question! What do you look like? Uh... like... are you like us, just like us, exactly or are there variations?

Haldra: From what I understand with humans, the average tends to be between five and six feet, this is very similar. Our averages is between five and six. But with your planet the understanding is that there are multiple colors, multiple types of individuals. Ones that range from very white to a very black, to even yellows and tans and browns. This is not how it works with us. The way that we have is only one specific color, and this is one that would be represented best in a light brown area or maybe a medium brown area. The colors you experience.

Jefferson: Right. And how tall did you say you are? Oh the same size as us... And what is the color of your eyes?

Haldra: We have green eyes and it is a type of green that is very light. Almost as a leaf that is just sprouting on one of your trees.

Jefferson: Wow. Do you get old?

Haldra: The physical body doesn't age. It only welcomes the inhabiting consciousness and releases it. And this is not a death process and it is not an aging process. It is when we are done with this specific existence, then we are ready to move to the next.

Jefferson: Hmm. How long can you live in your physical body?

Haldra: For us, it goes close to 700 of the years.

Jefferson: Oh. 700. And how old are you?

Haldra: 375, or maybe 76...

Jefferson: I was going to say... uh... I guess since you were born there were no women around right?

Haldra: Correct.

Jefferson: But aren't there women that come from other planets to visit you?

Haldra: Oh yes there is a variety of feminine races... uh... female in nature, coming from other places. Yes.

Jefferson: Don't you feel like hanging out with them, and making out?

Haldra: Uh... they are very attractive. The energy is quite different. So it is always a great experience to interact with them, physically, emotionally... in the energy.

Jefferson: Right. But you never make love to anybody.

Haldra: No. The sexual parts that the humans have are not needed for us.

Jefferson: What have you replaced that with?

Haldra: It looks as if there is a piece of skin that comes down. There is no definition or difference between this and the leg.

Jefferson: Oh you mean your genitals?

Haldra: Yes.

Jefferson: No, no... but I mean what have you replaced the sexual experience with?

Haldra: The sexual experience isn't needed for us. The sexual idea in exchange of energy is just this. And the entities who are sexual in nature, they exchange energy through a specific action. We do this but there is no sexual action needed.

Jefferson: So just let me see if I understand this, since you brought this up, the genitals that we have are different from yours... you don't have anything.

Haldra: Yes.

Jefferson: ...because you don't need it.

Haldra: Right.

Jefferson: Right. Okay. So do you wear clothing?

Haldra: Yes, we have things that cover the body. We wear thick and... uh... I am trying to think of a texture that would be a matching for you. Perhaps it would be similar to a wool but it is not made from animals.

***[Wool is the textile fiber obtained from sheep and certain other animals, including cashmere from goats, mohair from goats, qiviut from muskoxen, vicuña, alpaca, camel from animals in the camel family, and angora from rabbits. Source: Wikipedia]

Jefferson: And... so I would assume you don't make any trips to the toilet.

Haldra: No. Most entities that we come in contact with that are in the same density has no need to excrete waste because there is no waste that is released by the body. It is all used very well, it is an intricate system to do so.

Jefferson: So, do you have governments?

Haldra: We have structures that are built where there are

volunteers who assist the coordination of interactions with other entities, other species, other races and we do this with very few. And the rest of us facilitate in other ways. We do the exchanging of information, exchanging of resources for planets who are less abundant in a specific type of technology that we have and if they wish to change this type of technology, those who are starting in the beginning of fourth density, then we help exchange this and show them more efficient ways through technologies.

Jefferson: Are your cities the same as ours?

Haldra: Oh, yes. They are population centers; ones where many people meet at once. In a physical way, no. The appearance is nothing similar. I understand that in your planet, depending on what part or area you are on, the architecture and the fundamental building is different. For us it is very much the same. It is throughout the planet.

Jefferson: Do you have systems of transportation?

Haldra: Yes, we have three different transportation systems. We have ones that are on planet, to get it from one area to the next. We have one that is off planet, within short distances, within a ten light years (as it is what you would call to measure it) area, and we have large ones, much more people that are able to fit in there and go much further.

Jefferson: But do you also walk and run and swim?

Haldra: The swimming concept is not one that is valid on our race. A walking... this is done to move if we wish, as an experience but it is not necessary to facilitate movement.

Jefferson: If you were to walk amongst us, would we realize you are not from here?

Haldra: If you can experience me in the way that I am here, it would be very difficult for you to distinguish me from your fellow man.

Jefferson: In what way are you there then?

Haldra: In a higher vibrational level. I am not able to be experienced in the same way that you would be able to experience it, if I were vibrationally matching you.

Jefferson: So basically if you were to come to Earth and walk amongst us, we wouldn't see any difference because your race looks exactly like ours.

Haldra: Yes. I suppose this way you could see it but in fact I would be walking alone. I would not be able to experience you either. Because if I am walking on your planet, I am walking on a fourth density version of your planet.

Jefferson: Oh.

Haldra: Which has no physical human beings yet.

Jefferson: Have you been there yet?

Haldra: No. I have never made contact directly. All knowledge I have is of second hand nature.

Jefferson: What is your job in your race?

Haldra: My job is to take the transportation back and forth, within a ten light years area. I make contacts with all the races that surround us and... uh... it is hard to explain how relations are built, verbally, mentally, through energies. And I try to connect to all of these people so that if there is something within this area that can benefit our race, I will be one who has good rapport with them, enough to be able to facilitate exchanges.

Jefferson: Tell me one example of one thing that you found, in this area, that has already benefited your race, thanks to your interactions and contacts.

Haldra: If you want one specific example, the greatest example that I can give is through other race that is approximately five and one half light years from us. There was an exchange of technology. There is a crystalline substance that is of a very high vibration and this allows us to store more energy than the old ways that we used to have. We spoke many times. I was able to bring some of the delegates from our planets to interchange with the delegate from theirs, and the information and technology was exchanged and withing... a time period for you would be of one year, or approximately so. Everything that we had on our planet was then transformed from lower vibration crystals to smaller higher vibrating crystals. So this helped our race immensely.

Jefferson: Wow. And what is it about your race, that you have given to another race to help them in the same way.

Haldra: We have regiven the same gift of the smaller higher vibrating crystalline... But in a specific manner we have a very great substance that is used for conducting electricity. It is a very highly connective metal. More connective than even your ideas of lossless metal in your density because of the area of the molecules are compressed and very dense in yours, this is not so in ours. It is more widely distributed so that the electric flow is harder to come through. Because it is not as tightly connected and the electrons cannot contract with each other in such a manner. So to have a very highly zero loss connectivity metal it is very useful and our planet is abundant in this.

Jefferson: Wow. How does your system of education works for you?

Haldra: Education is a structure that is given by the delegates, they interact with the newly incarnated beings. And once they are interacting with them there is a certain amount of knowledge that is retained from one existence to the next and once they are incorporated back into these learning systems, perhaps schools, or colleges that you have... they are taught various things, and able to go and do as they wish. From this point going and train in one field or another.

Jefferson: So basically when you actually embody in your planet, you are already adults.

Haldra: Oh yes. The physical body is fully developed.

Jefferson: So you don't need to go through infancy stages?

Haldra: No. Our consciousness grows in between existences. Once it grows from one experience to the next, loosing some of the information there is expansion in the consciousness. And once this consciousness is fully expanded, than it is ready for physical existence.

Jefferson: Are you in the future?

Haldra: Uh... to your time... only 3 or 400 years. Approximately.

Jefferson: Do you have what we call religion?

Haldra: No. We understand that the universe is a function of something greater and that this functions is one of the... mechanics. One of laws. And we understand that this universe operates in a separate set of laws than other universes and we are well aware of this. The creating of this universe is made by other functions of larger structures. And this is well appreciated by us too. To connect to all of this is very entertaining and very enlightening. But to give it a religious idea or to believe that it is an entity that is higher than what we are able to achieve... It does not resonate with us.

Jefferson: How do you see God?

Haldra: God is that function.

Jefferson: Oh.

Haldra: It is the larger functions, rules... it is the systems that we work with within. And obviously we understand that there are greater aspects than the physical universe and in this non-physical, I suppose the connection that you get from going through the progression of a non-physical... this is what most ideas of gods are. So if we are to place a specific definition into God, then we place it at the highest level of the non-physical function.

Jefferson: Right. Like something such as... Supreme intelligence and first cause of everything.

Haldra: Correct.

Jefferson: Lovely. How do you relate to music?

Haldra: Music is only changing of vibrations. And it can... depending on the vibration... to depend on how we will resonate with this. For instance, ones that are very high in nature can give us an enlightening mood, can help us achieve the acts that we wish to do, the work that we are doing. It can help us achieve many things. But once this vibration is brought down to a lower degree, the sound is not only bringing our consciousness levels slightly down but it also gives us negative physical feelings.

Jefferson: So you already said you travel outside of your solar system. Right?

Haldra: Yes.

Jefferson: How do you do that?

Haldra: With our ships that we have.

Jefferson: What does it look like?

Haldra: It looks as a round sphere but the only thing that is different, besides being a sphere in shape, is the middle. There is an area that looks like an elongated rectangle which is placed around the middle of the sphere.

Jefferson: Wow.

Haldra: This is the one that I use to facilitate the ten light years... uh... the other ones are much larger. And they can no longer hold a circular shape. So they are more oblong. Much as your American football.

Jefferson: Oh.

Haldra: Yes. Understanding that football has many meanings in your planet, as well.

Jefferson: Right. How did you get this invitation?

Haldra: I was connecting to a higher version of myself. Perhaps to what you would say is a future version or a higher part of my consciousness. And when connecting to this, he was understanding that there is one, who looks like us, who wish to speak to us. And that they wanted to speak to us on the basis of the physical appearance... being similar. So that there is a greater understanding of how many, within the galaxy alone are possible to have looks that are very similar to yours. So I thought that this would be a great opportunity for me to speak to you.

Jefferson: So where were you when you got the message?

Haldra: I was at a dwelling of ours.

Jefferson: Oh, I see. Now, what do you know about Earth?

Haldra: I know various things. I know that your race is a... how would I explain this? Uh... It is a very strong race of incarnating beings. Uh... because they are going through cycles that are difficult, more difficult than most, therefore achieving levels of higher ability to manifest in a future physical incarnation and possibly going beyond the non-physical into higher physical existences or non-physical existences. I understand that there are many limitations that are set by a collective so that these are earned. ...that these abilities to manifest higher into the non-physical are earned by you. I know that there are many difficulties that are there. And now that I connect to the reptilian man [Treb] I am able to experience more of this. This is what I am doing as I speak to you. I experience many of your ideas and your history and your way of life now.

Jefferson: Am I the first human you talk to?

Haldra: In a human from your planet yes.

Jefferson: What about as in humans as in general?

Haldra: Uh... there are many races that do look like us.

Jefferson: Right, but that you have spoken with?

Haldra: Yes. If you say a human, means one from your planet, yes. The reptile is the one who thinks more of an idea of human being the way that we look. Uh... they are very different from the reptilian race but, looking in the same features that both of our races share. This is why I am trying to distinguish the meaning from you.

Jefferson: Right. What I mean is like... have you spoken to other races of human beings that look just like us, like your race and my race, that is in this galaxy?

Haldra: Oh yes. Many!

Jefferson: Which was the last race you spoke with? The last race?

Haldra: There is a race that is within the ten light years area.

And they are only two light years away from us and they are looking very much like us, but lighter as far as skin color and larger in height.

Jefferson: So you went to their planet?

Haldra: Yes. I have spoken to them, connected to them, many times.

Jefferson: What did you like the most about them?

Haldra: Uh... their ideas of fun and expressions that they choose to use for having fun... uh... they are very light hearted in nature. They do things, not so much because there is a function to do so but because they are enjoying it greatly to do some ways in what our race would say nothing. Doing absolutely nothing is joyous to them.

Jefferson: I know a race that sometimes go about their hours that way as well. It is called the Plenatalaka.

***[The Plenatalaka is a race of humans located in the Pleiades with whom we are currently in communication as well. Pleenaki is our Spokesperson. They look very much like us too and they are very light-hearted, fun and outgoing as well. Look out for the upcoming book with them.]

Jefferson: Is that the same one?

Haldra: No. This race is not the same race that you speak of. I am aware of this race that you speak of but it is not the same.

Jefferson: And have you visited this race I speak of?

Haldra: No. There has been no need. And this is well outside of a 10 light-years area. I am afraid that the ships that I use are not meant to go this far.

Jefferson: Okay. I will seat back and I will enjoy the messages that you have for our humans on Earth.

Haldra: Uh... it is a very short message but I want to express great love and great gratitude. I want there to be an understanding that even though your future seems to be unknown to you. It is only what you make it to be. Your race has probabilities of expanding in so many different ways and so many different outcomes that this is literally up to you as a collective consciousness of which one you want to choose. And as an individual sees this, as an individual understands this message, they will understand that they will have the possibility to go into a separate existence, as the one standing next to you. This is all a personal journey. One that will lead you far beyond your planet. And when you think that things are very hard or despair comes into you, remember this. Remember that you are expanding and that, for some races, pain or sorrow or suffering is the lesson that needs to be learned so that they are able to expand. And I wish to share this with you along with the great love of our race and thank you for connecting with us.

Jefferson: Wow. That was beautiful. Thank you very much. Did you enjoy sharing the message?

Haldra: Yes. It was very exhilarating to me.

Jefferson: Why?

Haldra: Because in the interaction of the in-formation, I have learned more of Earth just by connecting to this man and to this reptile than I have in the previous times of my 376 years that I have existed.

Jefferson: So, I am now part of your history!

Haldra: You are now part of my own history and also as a race, for communication with an Earth human.

Jefferson: So do you have an archive there? How is that... how is this conversation going to be part of your history?

Haldra: I am able to download this from my mindset into a machine that uses metal. The same kind we have abundance of and also crystals and it is given as an archive for our race's history.

Jefferson: Wow. Right. So write it down.. Capital letters: JEFFERSON VISCARDI, okay?

Haldra: Yes. We will do this.

Jefferson: Nah, I am just kidding! So... you say thank you very much, as well for your future self, who facilitated this connection to the reptilian that is connecting me through to you.

Haldra: Yes. I have done so and I will do this to yours as well.

Jefferson: Thank you. Now, how are you connecting to us? Are you... Do you have your eyes closed, are you under water?

Haldra: No there is a dwelling that I am staying at and then I am sitting on the place where we relax and sit and exchange information. And I am sitting here exchanging ideas and information.

Jefferson: So you don't need any machine to help you out?

Haldra: No.

Jefferson: And you don't need to be in a dark room.

Haldra: No.

Jefferson: Alright. Fantastic. That was it for today. I thank you very much and I wish you all the best. I hope that whenever a person reads this message you gave us, a rainbow of love and light appears in your skies.

Haldra: Thank you for this.

Jefferson: Good bye for now and thank you very much.

Haldra: Yes. Thank you very much as well.

Jefferson: Good bye Haldra.

SAULOYD HUMANS

Chapter 6
09/05/2012

Planet: Sauloyd
Lifespan: 1250 years

Spokesperson: Saul
Age: 971 years old

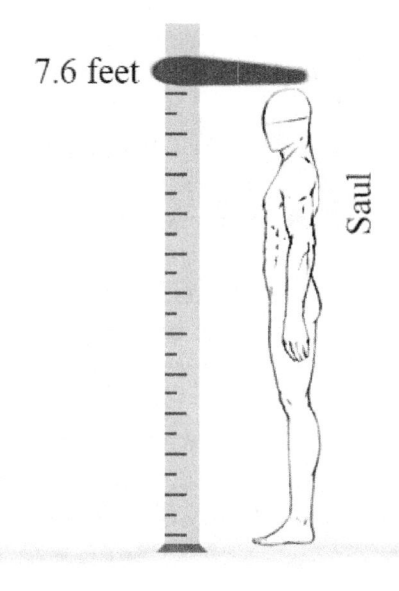

7.6 feet

Saul

Galactic Human: Hello Jefferson!

Jefferson: Yes.

Galactic Human: How are you doing?

Jefferson: I am doing great! Who am I having the satisfaction to speak with?

Galactic Human: We don't have representations. We don't have given names.

Jefferson: Oh.

Galactic Human: Uh... would you like me to give you one so it is easier to facilitate this?

Jefferson: Yes.

Galactic Human: Uh... Let's us call it Saul.

Jefferson: Okay. So, why don't you have name?

Saul: We don't use verbal communications. So there really is no need for a label or a tag to yell at, or to say the words to catch attention of. So it is more of a connection in a mental way.

Jefferson: Where are you right now?

Saul: I am on my planet.

Jefferson: But is there grass on the floor?

Saul: No. The area that I am at right now, is a very rocky place. We do have similar plants to grass, but it is not here.

Jefferson: Why are you there?

Saul: It is my job to be here.

Jefferson: Oh great we are going to talk about that later. Now... what constellation are you?

Saul: Uh... one second please...

***[Silence]

Saul: I've been told that the constellation name is a Majorus?...

Uh... Majoris!...

Jefferson: Majoris?

Saul: The dog Majoris.

Jefferson: The dog?

Saul: The dog of Majoris.

*** [Canis Major is one of the 88 modern constellations, and was included in the 2nd-century astronomer Ptolemy's 48 constellations. Its name is Latin for 'greater dog', and is commonly represented as one of the dogs following Orion the hunter (see also Canis Minor the 'lesser dog'). Canis Major contains Sirius, the brightest star in the night sky, known as the 'dog star', which is part of the asterism known as the Winter Triangle in the Northern Hemisphere, or the Summer Triangle in the Southern. The star is also recognized as Canis Major's nose. Source: Wikipedia.]

Jefferson: Okay and what planet are you from?

Saul: Uh... again we don't have the usual verbal... because I have given you a verbal representation of Saul. Let's call it Sauloyd.

Jefferson: Alright. And is your planet as big as ours?

Saul: Much smaller.

Jefferson: Wow. How long is a day for you?

Saul: In your time, if I am giving a mathematical translation...

uh... you have hours and days... uh... seventy six hours, maybe.

Jefferson: Wow. What is the color of your skies?

Saul: It is white.

Jefferson: Wow. Like... pitch (sheer) white?

Saul: Uh... no. Like a white white.

Jefferson: [Laughter] How many people do you have there?

Saul: We have twelve thousand.

Jefferson: That is it?

Saul: We are a very small race. But we have enough.

Jefferson: Do you have hurricanes, earthquakes, weather imbalances...

Saul: I am afraid that if we had a moving of the ground we would be in a lot of trouble from this little area.

Jefferson: [Laughter] Do you have bridges?

Saul: Bridges?...

Jefferson: Yes. It is like when you... you know, say there is a river that is going down its course and then you have to go to the other side. So you go over the bridge!

Saul: Oh no. Now I understand what you mean. We do not.

Jefferson: How do you do to go to the other side of a river?

Saul: [Giggles] There are no rivers that come through. We don't have liquid or standing water. Not in bodies. Perhaps a small part of them, maybe a few inches or a feet in diameter. But this is where it is coming up from the ground.

Jefferson: Oh. And how is your solar system set up?

Saul: Our solar system is a bit different than yours, if I understand it well. There is one large star and there are six planets that come around. And we are the sixth planet. But it is still very bright. If you think of your star, make it seventy, or seventy-five times larger. And we are probably twenty-five or thirty times further away from the star but it is still outshining the amount of light that comes into yours.

Jefferson: And all the planets go around the star in a circle... rot... rotating...

Saul: Not a perfect circle, but close. Yes.

Jefferson: And they rotate on their axis.

Saul: There is one planet that does not but the rest of them, yes.

Jefferson: And is your planet tilted to the side like ours?

Saul: It is not tilted the way yours is, but it is a much deeper angle.

Jefferson: So you do have seasons...

Saul: Uh... it is all the same weather. But the way that we face the Sun and how close we are, this is different. Yes.

Jefferson: Oh I see. What density are you?

Saul: We are in the fourth density.

Jefferson: Hey, how many moons do you have?

Saul: There are no natural satellites.

Jefferson: How are you guys born?

Saul: There is a 'sudo-sexual' manner. I am not sure if that is the right wording. It is a sexual manner but not the same with yours. Yours are two beings that come together, doing certain rituals of physical. And with us it is a two being that come together, but we do not have to use that same ritual. It is one that is more... exchanging of energy instead of fluids.

Jefferson: Oh I see. So how do women get to be pregnant?

Saul: The mechanism inside their body, allows them to have specific entities that are smaller but when we exchange energies, it brings one to the growth area. An area of growth inside. And it happens one at a time.

Jefferson: So you... you don't seed the body of the being that is going "to be born" into her womb.

Saul: No it is already inside of the womb. As an adolescent grows, one that is of the female nature, then they are also growing this twelve individual sex. And once they are at fully developed nature, then an exchange of energy can be made and the first one begins to grow bigger than the other. The eleven are fully developed and so is this but once this one grows, it grows larger and it is the only one that grows. So when this grows, it becomes a child and there is birth and then the next time that they wish to have a child, then they will go exchange energies and then the eleventh one will start to grow and then ten will remain. And this continues until all twelve are used.

Jefferson: Ohhhhh. Let me see if I understood. They have the womb and inside the womb they have twelve little seeds and those seeds are going to wake up every time you interact energetically.

Saul: Yes. But a seed, perhaps, would be a simple way to see it. Because it is a fully developed encasement or a body, it only grows further once the interaction of energy is exchanged.

Jefferson: Oh... so I was going to use the comparison of the pop corn in a microwave. So it is not like that at all?

Saul: Uh...

Jefferson: In a microwave you put the popcorn and then you put the energy... it pops!

Saul: Uh... yes but.. maybe if the popcorn that you use was already popped but it has just gotten larger.

Jefferson: Oh I see. So you already have a human physical body pre-developed but it is really, really tiny.

Saul: Yes. Maybe the size of a ball, the small one... a golf ball.

Jefferson: Wow. But how can the women fit twelve of those in her belly she may as well look fat.

Saul: They are not greatly taking up much space. The system that you use of a physical nature has many organs that are used to take away nutrition from there and redistributed accordingly. And very much of your lower abdominal areas are given to this waste facilitation and this isn't so with us. So there is much uh... back by the spine area.

Jefferson: So there is a lot of space there that you can use for these type of microwave oven human popcorns. [Giggles]

Saul: Yes.

Jefferson: Wow that is amazing. Okay and then, once you have this exchange of energy that you awaken that little thing to life, how long does it stay in her womb?

Saul: About the time of seven years of your time.

Jefferson: Right. And how does it come out?

Saul: Through an area that is lower, in between the leg area. The same as I would imagine... your race. Yes.

Jefferson: And then... when you have a child, what does it happen? Like... does it stay with the mother?

Saul: It is free to run around. We only have one major city on our planet and it stays in this area.

Jefferson: So, it doesn't really stay in the mom's house... does it need to be breast fed?

Saul: No. Nutrition is given to it the same way that we all

receive. And this is with the plant that we grow.

Jefferson: And how tall do you grow?

Saul: For a physical size, in between 7 and 8 feet.

Jefferson: How tall are you?

Saul: I am in between a seven and one half or slightly taller than one half.

Jefferson: What is your eye color?

Saul: We are all having the same eye colors. Either green or blue. And mine, specifically is blue.

Jefferson: Wow. Do you get old?

Saul: There is a process of energy that is not being used as well but it doesn't manifest physically. The bodily energy that we use isn't as efficient in the ages... uh... getting closer to the releasing of our consciousness. So it affects the... energy-wise inside of the body, but it doesn't manifest outward as most of the third density entities do, as they begin to release that consciousness.

Jefferson: You speak of releasing consciousness, do you believe in reincarnation?

Saul: Uh... it is not... It is not a belief, it is an understanding. I have recalled my previous existence since I have been on this planet.

Jefferson: So you know who you were in your last lifetime?

Saul: I have very great visual representations. Yes.

Jefferson: Were you an Earth human?

Saul: As far back as this I haven't looked outside of this life. I have a great connection to this planet. I understand that I have had existences before I was on this planet. But it doesn't interest me as far as to reach back this way.

Jefferson: Okay. How long can you live in your physical body?

Saul: For... Uh... I am imagining the time is 12 to 13 hundred.

Jefferson: Days.

Saul: Uh... of your years.

Jefferson: Yeah, I was just kidding. How old are you?

Saul: Personally, I myself am 971.

Jefferson: And do you have wife and kids?

Saul: We have many that we connect to. And because there is not many of us, we exchange energy with each other. So it is not like we connect with one and stay with them. But there are definitely ones that we prefer to be with... uh... for our conversations, emotion and energetic exchanges, yes.

Jefferson: Are men and women the same? Do they look the same?

Saul: No. The men are taller in size and the women tend to be slightly shorter.

Jefferson: And how are your muscles distributed in your body?

Saul: It is fairly similar to yours. If you see a regular Earth human... it is about the same size. Not the kind that lift up heavy things to make the muscles bigger, but an average built one.

Jefferson: Alright. Do you have governments?

Saul: No. We have a society that understands the importance of agreeing on things. So there is no need to give one person, ideas that can make others do what they do not wish to do.

Jefferson: [Laughter] Right. So... You do... Because government, sometimes, is the idea that the people decide what is good for everybody... (Sarcastic giggling)

Saul: And sometimes that doesn't work out so well for ones who don't resonate with those ideas.

Jefferson: Wow. That is terrible. I think if we put some enlightened scientists in strategic positions of "power", then they would care to direct the Earth's resources and our leading edge knowledge to the well-being of the entire humanity. What do you think about that idea?

Saul: Uh... I think that it is very great. Because you are giving the opportunity for many to be able to learn from those who have experience in manifesting the things that are needed and also be able to share them in a way that others understand. I think that is great.

Jefferson: Are your cities like ours?

Saul: We have one specific city and within this city... it is... uh... a very large area. So if you think of it from a perspective of yours, maybe you would see it as one building with many corridors.

Jefferson: It is... do you have like... windows, and stairs and elevators?...

Saul: There are places that we are able to look outside of the planet if you want to. There are special areas that you can go to look outside. Others prefer the bright light not to penetrate the wall so they tend to keep it closed off from the light. It is very, very... uh... if your human eyes were there it would be excessively blinding.

Jefferson: Hey, what is the color of your skin?

Saul: The color is very white. Almost to the idea of what... when I explained to you the color of the sky? This is very close. Our skin is... perhaps two decimal degrees lighter than that, if you are looking at a large wide spectrum.

Jefferson: Are you white like our humans are white or whiter?

Saul: The humans I understand to yours, are pink.

Jefferson: [Giggles] Right. Pink. No... no but... Well they are what we call white with some variations of color... but we are not pink... I mean... [Giggles]

Saul: Yes. I understand there are many colors but the ones you refer to as being white are more pink or pitch than they are white.

Jefferson: Right, so you are really white.

Saul: Yes. When I use the term white, it is a very literal interpretation of this color.

Jefferson: So if you were to walk amongst us, do you think we would be able to realize you are not from this planet?

Saul: If you are using your eyes, to look at us, yes. If we are able to be experienced by you, I do not believe there are many large, purely white humans that would be there. If you took our size, and if you took our skin color, and compare it, then yes. Perhaps you would see us as one of your own, but I do not think that we could be mistaken for a direct human.

Jefferson: Do you kiss one another?

Saul: During the energetic exchanges that produces children, it is a very close standing with the bodies touching at the front but it is not the same ideas as kissing, even though the face is touching each other.

Jefferson: Okay. So, you didn't answer... Do you have systems like elevators, and stairways in your cities?

Saul: Oh there are different levels, up and down. But they are very easily to walk. There is no need for machinery to pull you.

Jefferson: But, can you also jump? Jump high?

Saul: Yes. We can if we wish. The gravity is not nearly as dominant as it is in your planet. So we are able to jump but there is also the ability to move consciousness, instead of just the physical body. We are giving this extra... added element, to our existence.

Jefferson: Understood. Would you have systems of transportation?

Saul: There is only one. One way that we come and one way that we go. When we have to leave our planet because we have one city and one area, the rest of the way is easy moved from projection. But when we go outside of our planet, we do use technology.

Jefferson: What is your job and your passion in your planet... and are they both one and the same?

Saul: Oh yes. Job is an idea of something that you must do, in order to facilitate your own needs, but for us a job is something that you do that you love, that facilitates all needs. Not just the needs of yourself. And so there is a difference in definition. But if you want to see it from your definition of a job, or my job it is the same thing. It is a communication at a specific area of the planet. There is a large rock area and on this side... it is a cooler side with not as much sun directly given to it. So this is a reservoir of cooled water and air and sometimes we enjoy being... given this cool air and cool water. So I facilitate the moving of this from one place to the next.

Jefferson: Wow. In the beginning you said you were not in a place where you have grass. But you are in a place where you have water.

Saul: I was in a place... when I first spoke to you that was having rocks and below these rocks are the water and above this is the cooled air.

Jefferson: What about now? Are you at the same place?

Saul: Yes. I have not moved since we talked. Physical function must lessen when a communication of this magnitude is taking place. So I am stopping what I am doing at the time so that I can facilitate the communications.

Jefferson: Oh. I am very thankful for your taking off of your time to speak to our race.

Saul: Oh, this is a great pleasure of mine.

Jefferson: So what is your job?

Saul: To move the cool air and water to the other places. It is set up in a line, one that is round. And I am able to manipulate the pump that does this. I guest this is the best description, a pump. And it pushes it closer to the city.

Jefferson: Why is that needed?

Saul: For people who wish to splash in water and for people who are too heated when they come to the housing side areas. This place tend to be a little cooler and when we pump the water it cools down the air in a separate shaft and this also belongs to the city.

Jefferson: Isn't it boring?

Saul: No. I find great joy interacting with this water. There are many small life elements in this. And they communicate but in a way that is... most people on your planet would probably not understand. Because this is such a small degree of interaction, for... a term or an expression that you might understand better, is to watch grass grow or to watch paint dry. Most humans say: "this is very boring" or "a waste of time".

Jefferson: Right.

Saul: But for us it is a great interaction. A great energetic reaction. Even if I place water on my hand and it sits still. There is still movement within the energy, there is still consciousnesses that are in this water. And to be able to feel it gives me such a great joy.

Jefferson: Do you have systems of education?

Saul: Oh, we are always learning things from each other. In the cities there is what you would probably call open hours, or open times... where people speak of what they love. If you want to learn about this, then you come to this area, inside the city and you listen. And it is so great to hear other's experiences and knowledge of love.

Jefferson: Can I go there? You are inviting!

Saul: Uh... if you are able to close your eyes. You can come here now!

Jefferson: [Giggles] Yes. But then I would have to go through my belief systems that tell me I would be able to only imagine myself going there but not really go there.

Saul: It seems to be interesting the idea of imagining. Uh... and the idea of belief systems that don't allow you. If you are able to believe that you are speaking to someone who is very, very far away from you, this is not any less believable than being able to come and see us with your own soul. It runs on the same applications of rules...

Jefferson: Yeah... not really. Because when I am talking to you I know that there is this reptilian being [Treb] that is connecting to the channeler [Rob], who has the ability to connect to other races. Which we all have to some degree, but some have it more intensified, to the point of being able to connect outside. But then, that is something pretty much possible and even natural. But it is also natural for me to imagine but it is not natural for me to say that my imagination is real. I could be making it up!

Saul: I see. So would it help if I connected the reptilian to you?

Jefferson: [Giggles] I would probably be scared to death! I think this is like... uh... a process. You know? Like... one that we each have to go through in order to acclimate to that point where we are a match to that reality. Do you understand?

Saul: Oh this is very fascinating!

Jefferson: Oh, why... [Laughter]

Saul: To see the way that you have to grow through these ideas.

Jefferson: I know, it is terrible!

Saul: It is fascinating.

Jefferson: No it's terrible.

Saul: No, it is not terrible. It is an experience of learning.

Jefferson: [Giggles] I know right? So are you going to share that later on to your people there?

Saul: Oh yes! They are sharing in one way or another now. They understand what I am doing here. And many of them are choosing to listen now, and some will choose to listen later, when it is my time to speak at the teaching facility. This will be what I speak of next!

Jefferson: Fantastic. So yeah. I mean. it is pretty fascinating how we can definitely believe that you are there and you are talking to me because of the human physical ability, given by the soul's theme in this particular life time, in the case of the channeler. Where he has this... more expanded, extended energy in his connection body and soul that allows him to pick up on signals from other places and then through this medium I can definitely communicate to you.

    I can talk to a disembodied human... uh... you know? So that is perfectly fine, but then when we go to our imagination... uh... we've learned that the imagination is just not important. Although... [Laughter] I know we are completely wrong by the studies I've made and by people like you that have taught us. But yes. Definitely. Imagination is just something that you make up; it is not something that you should believe. And if you do believe everything you imagine, to the point of letting it make you behave in a particular way, then we take you to the hospital where we treat crazy people.

Saul: This is so amazing! Uh...

Jefferson: [Giggles]

Saul: While you speak of this a thought process has come through that the children on your planet still use this imagination to benefit their lives daily.

Jefferson: Absolutely!

Saul: What happens from children to adult?

Jefferson: Well, what happens is that we acclimate to the external environment demands, which makes us think and believe as if we belonged to a society where we all have to work for others [to compete over resources] and basically become a well adjusted person in a sick society.

Saul: Absolutely brilliant!

Jefferson: So in that sense we have the same process I spoke to you about before of growing through a process and acclimating to the idea where you come from having that expanded mind-consciousness system, from the time we are born until you are five, and then by the time you are seven, you are already pretty much 'dumbed' down, formatted to be just another mouth speaking and another body working.

Saul: I see. [sadly spoken]

Jefferson: Yeah... It is... no... it is fascinating and sad at the same time. But you know, time will tell. Time takes everything it gives!

Saul: You are a fascinating 'explainer' of these ideas. And I want to just express to you that this happens for a reason so that you are able to grow greatly. Within this type of environment, room for growth is exploding from every floor.

Jefferson: Yes absolutely! I understand there is organization behind this and there is a greater meaning; absolutely. Yeah. Yes. But coming back to our conversation... uh... so there is no way that I can go there and visit you, because my imagination and the process of acclimating to the idea to believe that and just... for us just to imagine that I am at your planet is not enough. What I would like to, is that you would manifest yourself or your craft here in our planet. And uh... you just call me before and then I go and then you take me and then I visit your planet! That way!

Saul: This is a lovely idea! Uh... the Treb Bor yit-NE explains that your race is still in the growing, and development stages?

Jefferson: Yes.

Saul: This is true as well?

Jefferson: Yes. Absolutely! It is true! We are the "psycho dudes" in quarantine!

Saul: Perhaps when this comes, when your race has grown to this, then perhaps we will be able to facilitate such a meeting.

Jefferson: Right. So go ahead and have a visit to Pleenaki and then... he will come here in thirteen to ten years, then you come with him.

Saul: This will be a great experience!

Jefferson: Deal?

Saul: It sounds like this is great.

Jefferson: Fantastic. Then, let me focus here in this book's idea... do you guys have religion on your planet?

Saul: No. There is no religion.

Jefferson: What is the meaning of life for you?

Saul: To grow, to expand and experience all at the same time.

Jefferson: How do you see God?

Saul: We see God as a place of energy who distributes this energy, out, in various ways and then in exchange for this energy we give him an idea, an intimate picture of what it is to go through our experience. So it is an exchange from a greater density entity to us. From one of energy and exchange of experience. And that is a great exchange.

Jefferson: So what you are saying is the One is the All and the All are the One!

Saul: Yes. That is a good way to say it.

Jefferson: Would you agree that God then is what we could name as supreme intelligence and first cause of everything?

Saul: Oh yes. Uh... he is the one who has facilitated every part of energy that makes us up. Not only in a physical sense but also in a soul sense or a non-physical sense. And yes, he is the one who facilitates every action, reaction and everything that happens as we experience it. And we trade this experience for the energy he gave us to allow us to go through our own experiences, first hand.

Jefferson: How do you guys relate to music?

Saul: Music is a great part of our society. There are several instruments that are being played. And once they are being played, it gives us all great joy to dance and to yell... much like singing.

Jefferson: Okay. How did you get this invitation?

Saul: I was feeling an energy that came into our system and we all sat to connect to it, and I specifically wished to make this interaction once we knew that the energy was wanting to speak to us and I specifically asked to do this.

Jefferson: Did you ask whom?

Saul: The energy that came. Now I understand that to be the one you call Treb.

Jefferson: Oh I see. Uh... what do you know about Earth?

Saul: There are many things that we understand. The physical aspects of it. The area that it resides in. There are many ideas, but speaking to you has given me a renewed sense of what it really is. Just as... uh... I am trying to think of a way to explain... A telephone game! Where you speak into the speaker and the next speaker is speaking, and then the one... after several times the information is not given quite in the way it starts. This is how it works with the word of mouth and energy exchanges between other races that don't understand the ways of each other.

Jefferson: So basically you had a different idea and now you have a much clearer idea about our society.

Saul: Oh yes. Much clearer!

Jefferson: Wow. So, are you ready to share with us your message?

Saul: If you allow me to, I would love to say a few words to you.

Jefferson: I am most excited to, not only allow you to but to sit back and listen to it really carefully! Thank you very much. Go ahead.

Saul: Thank you very much. The idea that your race has very, very hard limitations that you place in yourselves should not be something that discourages you. From our race, when I was explaining to what degree your race removes yourselves from your own belief systems within the younger ages to the older. How outside influences, acclimation of ideas of what should and should not be that make such a profound change in your existence from childhood to adulthood... I beg of you! That if you want to have an existence that is free of these limitations, revert yourself back into this child. Use this imagination that the children knew. Use the ideas of being able to aimlessly do everything without possibility of being able to stop. And I believe that if you incorporate this in each existence, then you will be so much happier as a race. That your growth will be so great that you will no longer have to see yourself as limited. And if you can do this, I wish for you to express this to everyone you know and share these ideas in great magnitudes with multiple people. I think that this would be a very big part for your race to grow. And this is the message that I will share for now.

Jefferson: Just like they say: "If you want to become enlightened... lighten up!" [Laughter]

Saul: [Giggles] Yes. That is very greatly said.

Jefferson: Wow. So I enjoyed this interaction immensely. How did you enjoy connecting and sharing your message?

Saul: Very well. This has been a very great excitement.

Jefferson: Fantastic. Thank you very much. You have a great time.

DROHN-ONDAHG HUMANS

Chapter 7
09/06/2012

Planet: Drohn-ondahg
Lifespan: 1100 years

Spokesperson: Mohj Ladrie
Age: 444 years old

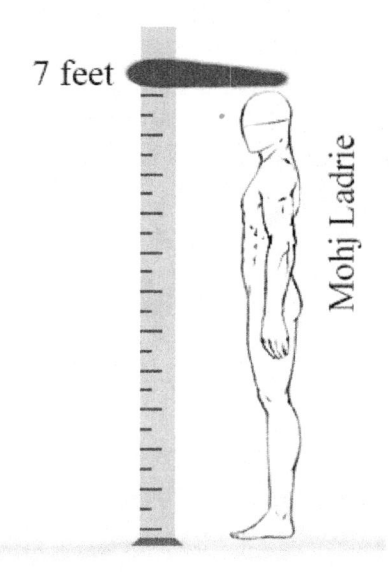

7 feet

Mohj Ladrie

Galactic Human: Hello?

Jefferson: How are you, there?

Galactic Human: I am doing fine and how are you doing?

Jefferson: It is lovely to speak to you, from Earth to... what is... who are you?

Galactic Human: My name is [a´9wu8r q´0].

Jefferson: Would you say it again please?

Galactic Human: Yes. Mohj Ladrie

Jefferson: Alright. So... Nice to meet you! What is your constellation?

Mohj Ladrie: From the stars and the situation in your skies? Rochealhead.

Jefferson: Where about is that? The dog? The dolphin? The kite?

Mohj Ladrie: I believe it is a woman with a snake.

Jefferson: Oh I see. And how do you name it again?

Mohj Ladrie: I believe it would be pronounced RohShiel-a-howd or hay... Roshiel-hay?

Jefferson: Oh I see. And what is the name of your planet?

Mohj Ladrie: The race of our people and planet are known throughout the rest of the galaxy as the Drohn-Ondahg

Jefferson: Okay. So that is the name of your race. And what is the name of your planet?

Mohj Ladrie: Uh... It is the same.

Jefferson: Okay. How long is a day for you there?

Mohj Ladrie: A day?... in the cycle of the planet?

Jefferson: Yeah. How long does it take for your planet to turn around itself once?

Mohj Ladrie: From one turn?... Two and one third of your days.

Approximately!

Jefferson: Uh huh. More or less?

Mohj Ladrie: Uh... two and one third of your days is one of ours, approximately.

Jefferson: Okay. Alright. What is the color of your skies?

Mohj Ladrie: Our skies?

Jefferson: Yeah.

Mohj Ladrie: It is a variance of orange and red color.

Jefferson: Wow. And when you come from outside what is the color of the planet?

Mohj Ladrie: It is the same. The atmosphere is very thick it gives a similar color coming from the outside.

Jefferson: How many people are there in your planet?

Mohj Ladrie: About one point two billion.

Jefferson: Wow. Is that bigger than ours or smaller?

Mohj Ladrie: The population is much smaller.

Jefferson: And the planet?

Mohj Ladrie: The size of the planet itself?

Jefferson: Yes.

Mohj Ladrie: Uh... it is larger than yours but not very much. Maybe one and one fourth or one and one fifth larger.

Jefferson: How is your solar system set up?

Mohj Ladrie: The way that our system works, is that there are two stars in the middle of the system, that are both... I consider it to be small red stars and we are traveling around both of it. There are several planets... 13. And the way that our planet is set, we are the fourth. There are many moons on every planet, besides the first and the last. And ours has two moons.

Jefferson: How many moons do you have around your planet again?

Mohj Ladrie: Two.

Jefferson: And what color are they?

Mohj Ladrie: One carries similar atmosphere to ours. It is only slightly dimmer in the orange-red color. And the other is a very dark rock... So, perhaps, dark-gray and black at some points.

Jefferson: What density are you?

Mohj Ladrie: We are in the fourth density.

Jefferson: How are you guys, from your society born?

Mohj Ladrie: We are born through a sexual nature.

Jefferson: I see. So, it is just like the human being... like you have dad's seed and mom's egg and then it grows in the womb for a certain amount of time.

Mohj Ladrie: Oh yes.

Jefferson: How long is that time?

Mohj Ladrie: Approximately one and one point of your years. So if your years are divided into twelve increments, correct?

Jefferson: Yes.

Mohj Ladrie: So, one and one increment.

Jefferson: Oh I see. So once you are born, you are breast fed, right?

Mohj Ladrie: There is no feeding from the actual mother as your race does this. There is a feeding of sustenance that is given to us when we are younger and once we reach an age of approximately ten of your years. Then we are able to eat different foods.

Jefferson: I see. So, do you divide your years into childhood, teenagerhood and adulthood?

Mohj Ladrie: There are several stages. There is the initial stage where you would be born and then becoming older, growing in size. Another stage would be where the body's function is of a complete nature. The third stage is a growing of consciousness of two ideals of all mathematical, all scientific information and then there is another stage after this, the fourth stage: where you are growing your ability to learn things outside of what is needed and after this it is considered to be a 'completed' entity.

Jefferson: But how... can you separate those stages in years, by ages?

Mohj Ladrie: The first age it is the same of being born and growing physically into the body and functions and this will be the first ten years. After this, is a growing into a complete nature, of being able to understand certain functions. This would be thirty years. Functions of the math and all the things that are needed. After this, approximately thirty years. Would be in the age of growing out to do things that are beyond what you wish to do. Beyond what you need to do. And after this, any time after this, then you are able to take this into effect and grow as you wish.

Jefferson: Wow. And... uh... how old are you now, then?

Mohj Ladrie: My age is approximately 444 of your years.

Jefferson: And how long do you live in your physical bodies?

Mohj Ladrie: About 1100.

Jefferson: So you are in what stage? All grown!

Mohj Ladrie: Yeah, I am at the stage of a complete entity.

Jefferson: Oh yeah. That is truth. You already have... uh... Okay... and... what do you guys look like?

Mohj Ladrie: We are very similar to your race in appearance: facial appendages... also having a wider build than yours but mostly we are similar in this way. We have long hair, that is black. We have skin that is very light, perhaps a medium tan or a light pitch, in between this.

Jefferson: How tall are you?

Mohj Ladrie: I am 7 feet.

Jefferson: And what is your eye coloration?

Mohj Ladrie: Mine is brown.

Jefferson: Why, do you have different sizes and eye colors there?

Mohj Ladrie: There are many different colors of eyes, depending on one soul and how it manifests itself outward.

Jefferson: It depends on the soul?

Mohj Ladrie: Yes. The soul gives all physical characteristics to the entities that are manifesting itself outwardly. Yes.

Jefferson: But can you change it during your lifetime?

Mohj Ladrie: If you wish to, yes.

Jefferson: So basically you can have your eyes to look green.

Mohj Ladrie: If this was a deep seated belief of mine I would be able to do this, yes.

Jefferson: Oh, I see. It is just like if it was a deep seated belief of mine I could just have my biology to respond to that.

Mohj Ladrie: Correct!

Jefferson: Oh okay. Yeah. Just... the difference is that in the fourth density that this might be easier.

Mohj Ladrie: Yes. There is less limiting energetic filters and also less understanding in your density of the resistance that we can give ourselves with the beliefs.

Jefferson: So what you are explaining me is that the barriers... the existing barriers for me to change my eye color is not of a physical nature.

Mohj Ladrie: No it is one of a non-physical. For example... if your race tends to see that you are born with a specific eye color in this phase then this is a very large, integrated collective belief. So this keeps your eye color the same from the time you are born and you tend to see that it comes from genetic. So you are giving yourselves odds and averages mathematically and some subconsciously built to see which appropriate eye color would come from the genes, and which you are born in. And this is all done subconsciously before you are born. Once you are born the soul takes the most resonating idea within the limitation of the probability and creates this.

Jefferson: I think it goes the same way with the aging idea, isn't it?

Mohj Ladrie: Yes there is much harder aging in the body of your race than there is with most others outside of the third density.

Jefferson: How does it work in your race? Do you guys get old?

Mohj Ladrie: We get to the end of our cycles and there are less, physical... uh... activities that we can do because we, our bodies become weak. It is because our consciousness is given away at certain points of our life. When they are not fully invested into things, portions of our consciousness are taken off and put into these things. So as we go, we are giving our consciousness a weight to all things that we do therefore lessening the amount that we are able to do, which makes a physical function less 'acceptable' or less... uh... I am not sure of the word that would use for this... less...

Jefferson: ...expressive!

Mohj Ladrie: Yes.

Jefferson: Uh huh. Now if I look at you today or if I look at you before you make your transition, will you look the same?

Mohj Ladrie: I will look the same as most part of the physical aspects, but there will be small portions of myself that will change because my energy is changing and when my energy is changing my physical appearance changes. It does not change in a way that your race does with the degradation, with the ailments or the negative connotation of physical breaking down but it changes in a different way, it changes in a way of experience and also of pure manifestation inside us.

Jefferson: Perhaps the depth in your eyes is a little different too?

Mohj Ladrie: Oh yes. Most of your race that I understand sees death as an end to a life. Most people tend to be sad about this or upset. And with us we understand it is a transitioning into the next existence. There is not much loss in between. You have to have somewhat of a clean slate when it comes to this transition because you are needing to have a new experience.

And if you keep your every thought of who you were in your previous incarnation then you can no longer have a new experience because you are still set in the same mindset which you were in the previous.

Jefferson: Uh... I was going to ask back then... if the look in your eyes... the depth is changed rather than the outside looking, because you grow wiser and not older.

Mohj Ladrie: Oh! Yes. The eyes are one manifestation of this and so is the rest of the body.

Jefferson: Okay. Now, are men and women the same?

Mohj Ladrie: Uh... well, they are different energetically and partially physically.

Jefferson: Well physically they are different in that they have different genitals but is it that the breast area is different too?

Mohj Ladrie: Uh... there is no change in the breast area from man to woman because it is no longer needed to feed the children.

Jefferson: Oh I see. So what makes a woman look different from a man?

Mohj Ladrie: They are having different genitals as you explained.

Jefferson: Right.

Mohj Ladrie: They are also having more extravagant pigmentation. It tends to be much richer in color.

Jefferson: Nice. Do you wear clothing?

Mohj Ladrie: Yes. We wear certain clothings.

Jefferson: Uh... do you have toilet trips?

Mohj Ladrie: Uh... Toilet trips?... I am not sure what is meant by this.

Jefferson: If you have to go and pee or do you have to take care of any waste that your body produces?

Mohj Ladrie: Oh, no. The waste has been taken care of long ago in the beginning of the mid transition. How you see a fourth density mid transition?... The body changes from generation to generation so you are no longer needing to waste material.

Jefferson: Alight. Do you kiss one another?

Mohj Ladrie: Uh... kissing?... No! This is not a ritual that we use.

Jefferson: Do you do anything instead of kissing... different?

Mohj Ladrie: To show affection for each other?... We would touch with hands, touch faces or of the eyes, and hold the energy to them. We give them all of our energy in transference of affection.

Jefferson: Wow. Do you guys have government?

Mohj Ladrie: We have structures that are set up with different working aspects, different jobs or things that you can do. But this is not a government set up in the way that perhaps you would think of it. For your governments there are ones you wish to be in command of the rest or one that are supposed to elect to a position of power who does things for the benefit of the rest, and as you have seen that this can cause problems when the one who you elected have different ideas than you. So, for us there are groups of ones that deals with specific affairs off world. But our planet still runs quite efficiently by itself. There is no need for dictatorship about what to do and how to do it. It is very easily and done without much resistance.

Jefferson: Are your cities like ours?

Mohj Ladrie: In what way do you mean?

Jefferson: Uh... in a way of constructions and buildings and transportation?

Mohj Ladrie: There are similar aspects to all. The traveling we do is short traveling. We have no need to go outside of the cities unless we wish to go to other places and visit other people. So when we are traveling around the areas that we have, we are able to project consciousness into whatever are that we wish. If we go further along the planet, they have an underground system that is able to take you where you wish to go quite quickly and then we also have craft that go off world. And when the off-world crafts are gone, there are many different kinds, but we have several.

Jefferson: Thank you. And what is your job and, or passion in your race? Are both one and the same for you?

Mohj Ladrie: Yes. I have many passions that are outside of what I do to help others but I would say it is my greatest passion, yes. And this passion is to facilitate communications outside of our planet.

Jefferson: Wow. So do you have people like myself that go to you and ask you to connect to other people like a channeler?

Mohj Ladrie: This is one way that communication is done. There is also verbal communication, there is also technological communication. There are many types. But yes this is very probable.

Jefferson: So you are a translator too. You are not only an ambassador. Do you also translate to other races to talk to your race?

Mohj Ladrie: Well translation requires two different mediums and understanding of the change in information to clear those. With us it is slightly different from this. It is a pure communication of conscious thought in a technological aspect of this. Whatever signal they are receiving it is already given in that way that they can understand. It is pre-translated from their technology. The database within the galaxy is very large. So most of the written communication is done by itself. It is translated into ideas that they understand.

Jefferson: Right.

Mohj Ladrie: ...with no need for me to facilitate that specifically.

Jefferson: How does your education system works?

Mohj Ladrie: It is learning. People sit and teach the other people what they want to know. In a more specific idea, there are much questions that the younger ones have. But as far as teaching them things that they need to know, this is done vibrationally. So if... uh... let's say a child would walk and seeing people doing things he will have a natural understanding of this telepathic connection to them. But the more specific details, if they are not surrounded by one who knows this, then they are able to send out a verbal or mental communication that allows them to receive it back.

Jefferson: Oh, I see. It is all done through telepathy.

Mohj Ladrie: Much of it is. There is still spoken words. There is still a spoken language but it is not used nearly as the telepathic.

Jefferson: Alright. Do you have religion?

Mohj Ladrie: What is the definition that you hold of religion?

Jefferson: Religion is when you allow yourself a time to reconnect to a being that is outside of what you are and where you exist in order for you to experience self transcendence.

Mohj Ladrie: I am not sure that definition quite fits.

Jefferson: I know. [Laughter]

Mohj Ladrie: Well for our race. This is what I mean.

Jefferson: Ah okay. [Giggles]

Mohj Ladrie: For our race we connect to many entities that are outside of our self for gathering information and enlightenment. But it is... transcendence is an idea that is our life own building. It is a transcendence from birth until the end of our existence. So, all the time we are transcending ourselves.

Extraterrestrial Life

So I am not sure that this idea of the definition would fit us but the rest could. There are many such as the one that is connecting to you now. The Treb man is connecting to me often and also gives me great information and inspiration.

Jefferson: Yeah. The definition most... a wider definition of religion in our planet is that you go to... it is an organized institution that wants you to see the world through their eyes in order to... for many reasons. For believing in a particular way, different from other people; some do that to get money from other people and make them their subject of... not enslavement but something of that order. So religion is most seen as that, different... divergency... different ways to look at an external God that they believe can save us by behaving good.

Mohj Ladrie: Uh... now, this definition is quite opposite. Uh... To be saved?... uh... I am not quite sure of the idea behind this but I imagine that it means to have your life changed in a way by someone else? Is this what you mean?

Jefferson: To be saved means when you die you don't go to hell, you go to heaven!

Mohj Ladrie: Where is hell and heaven?

Jefferson: Hell is the place where there is a being, supposedly created eternally to go against God's will and make you pay for disobeying God's words translated by human beings. [Giggles] But... uh... and heaven is a place where you are eternally doing nothing. You are just scratching your asses and lying around and playing harp. Just doing nothing. It is they way they believe.

Mohj Ladrie: Well... uh...

Jefferson: The right word is: contemplating the greatness of God. [Giggles]

Mohj Ladrie: This is a quite different idea from how we experience things. Mostly it is a rationalization mechanism to understand things that they believe they are not great enough to understand. Perhaps this is why is this a thought. But I assure you, everyone who is incarnated physically, whether it is from a stone or whether it is the highest of the physical existences, all are great enough to not have to be save. They are great enough to exist. Therefore they are a part of this external God, imagining this is the idea of creation itself. So, yes I understand and we do not have that here.

Jefferson: Okay so how do you see God?

Mohj Ladrie: We understand it as a source of energy. That is creation. It is more than an entity. It is everything. It is a multi-layered, multi-dimensional and also multi-understanding... uh... multiple levels of understanding this. It is everything that is. It is also outside of everything that is. And it is a part of everything that is. It is the energy that we are.

Jefferson: Okay. Fantastic. So, can I also say that it is the supreme intelligence and first cause of everything?

Mohj Ladrie: Yes. This will fit quite well into our seeing.

Jefferson: Fantastic. I guess it is time for you to share with us your message. Just before: are you in the future?

Mohj Ladrie: Uh... in the future?... the time line? This is what you want to know?

Jefferson: Yeah.

Mohj Ladrie: 1300 years ahead of you.

Jefferson: Alright. So would you feel free then, now to share with us your message please?

Mohj Ladrie: Yes. I am grateful to connect to you and your people. There are many things that can be learned from exchanges of this way. It is understood that there are many different ideals on your planet. Many different ways of life and before you are ready to express your great want of connection to outside of your planet, first you must do this through your own planet. You must take the time to understand the ones who are next to you. Who you could not understand before you must take it within your mind to reach and cross the barrier that you set in language, or religion, or idealisms. Even in physical borders that you have that divide you.

    You must breach this. Everyday from an understanding of your planet this is worked upon. Some work it on one way and some on the other. But there is still to be progression either way you look at this. Continue your progression in the way that you need to, so that you can have a better understanding of your own self and your own race and your own people. And when this happens you will be able to achieve connections to many others. There are hundreds of thousands of races that are specifically waiting for you to be done fighting amongst yourselves so that we may introduce ourselves. If you finally become amongst yourselves eventually able to connect to those ones in your race and be able to appreciate the differences instead of to denounce them or to personify them with stereotype ideas that you have. Then you will be able to understand them in a great way and be able to understand yourSelf in a greater way. All that you need, all that you believe is of... and all that you come in contact with are really only an external manifestation of what is happening inside of you. So if you see someone to be faulted or if you see someone to be different it is because you are having differences and faulted energies within yourself. So creating this connection to them would be beneficial so that you will be able to connect outside your own planet. We are waiting to continue our communication with you and thank you for the opportunity!

Jefferson: Thank you very much! Uh... how did you get this invitation?

Mohj Ladrie: As it is my job to communicate and to facilitate all external... not all but much of it. The one that you know to be Treb man, he is the one who has connected to me and asked if it was appropriate to connect to me for me to talk to you and to facilitate this communication. And it was a brilliant idea.

Jefferson: So it was through telepathy.

Mohj Ladrie: Yes. I have not met this Treb man in a physical sense. Only through a communication that is non-physical.

Jefferson: Right and now... I am part of your history, right!?

Mohj Ladrie: Oh yes. This is the very first contact through this mechanism... uh... channeling idea from Earth.

Jefferson: Do you guys keep an archive of things?

Mohj Ladrie: There is a knowledge that is ingrained in all of us. It is a part of our birth and it is a part of our society. This is one of the stages, of growth that we go through as we are being integrated with all of the ideas in the telepathic way.

Jefferson: So what I mean I think, is that if someone wants to listen to our conversation of today, how would they go about doing that?

Mohj Ladrie: It will be directly broadcasted from my memory to theirs.

Jefferson: Oh okay. Fantastic. So thank you very much. It was lovely meeting you and talking to you and learning from you. Okay?

Mohj Ladrie: Yes. That was great to connect to you too. And I am very grateful that you are giving time to exchange informational ideas.

Jefferson: Okay so Mr. Mohj Ladrie, thank you very much and you have yourself a wonderful life.

Mohj Ladrie: You do this as well.

KALAMEELU HUMANS

Chapter 8
09/06/2012

Planet: FramAnehl
Lifespan: 1500 years

Spokesperson: Tassasol
Age: 298 years old

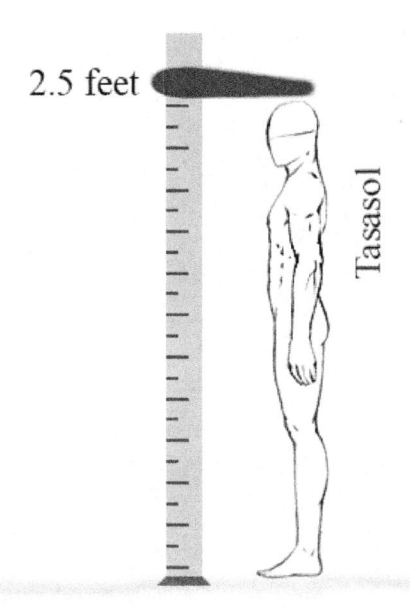

2.5 feet

Tasasol

Galactic Human: Greetings Jefferson?

Jefferson: How is your day there in your planet, right now?

Galactic Human: It is very exciting!

Jefferson: Excitement is shared on the same level but for having the opportunity to speak with you.

Galactic Human: This is why it is exciting for me as well. So it seems that we have shared this common excitement.

Jefferson: [Giggles] Who are you my friend?

Galactic Human: My name is Tassasol

Jefferson: Alright. So, what constellation are you?

Tassasol: I am not sure the constellations names. One moment.

***[Silence]

Tassasol: It is a double fish.

Jefferson: Oh, Pisces.

Tassasol: Uh… yes! This is correct.

Jefferson: So, what is the name of your planet?

Tassasol: Our planet's name is FramAnehl

Jefferson: Okay. What is the size of your planet? Is that as big as ours?

Tassasol: Uh… it is bigger than yours. I am not sure quite… how large yours is… with an understanding, I suppose it is approximately eight or nine times the size.

Jefferson: Wow. That is pretty big!

Tassasol: Yes.

Jefferson: How long is a day for you?

Tassasol: A day for us is within nine hours of yours.

Jefferson: So you move pretty quick.

Tassasol: Compared to some, yes.

Jefferson: What is the color of your skies?

Tassasol: When you look up, it is a blue light, orange.

Jefferson: How many people do you have there?

Tassasol: Approximately 700 million.

Jefferson: When you are coming from outside of the planet, what does the planet look like?

Tassasol: If you are coming from the outside, it appears to be very blue, in appearance. If you are coming from far out, when you get closer you will see that blue is a color but also having parts of red.

Jefferson: Can you speak about your solar system set up?

Tassasol: Solar system set up?... Are you meaning the amount of stars and planets within it?

Jefferson: Yes. And how they are placed... perhaps it is just like ours, but this is just so we can understand it.

Tassasol: There is a very large star compared to yours. Maybe three or four times the size of yours and then there is also a smaller star. This is a very, very small red star. And these starts interact with each other. It appears, from an outside perspective perhaps that the small red star is moving around the larger one but it is not true. They are only sharing a similar point of gravity so the larger star is still moving slightly but the other one comes around it. Within this system there are 15 planets. Each planet has an independent orbit which does not cross any other planet orbit. There are several hundred moons around the planets and we are located within the fifth planet. And then in this fifth planet, orbiting around us, we have 12 moons.

Jefferson: Why do you have so many moons?

Tassasol: The body of the planet itself is very large. It attract many of the smaller portions that were not able to be pulled outside of the gravitational area of our planet. They are all very small with exception of three. Most of them are considered to be, in your measurements, only a few hundred kilometers across.

Jefferson: Wow. It must be exciting to look up the skies!

Tassasol: Yes. It is very beautiful.

Jefferson: What density are you?

Tassasol: We are in the fourth density.

Jefferson: So how are you guys born?

Tassasol: We are born from a process... uh... I am trying to see a word that is appropriate...

Jefferson: uh huh.

Tassasol: Perhpas... bud?

Jefferson: Bud? [Like flower bud?]

Tassasol: It is a process where genetics are places in the body, in the physical body and then an area in the stomach region of the females, once a sexual interaction has happened, protrudes on the stomach, creating a small ball [the bud]. This small ball is removed and placed into an environment, which keeps the temperature regulated, and once this temperature regulates, then the child is born.

Jefferson: I see. Oh. So it is a process of extraction of the fertilized egg from the women's womb and then you have an "in-vitro" growth.

Tassasol: Uh... Well, more precisely, I suppose, it is better explained that there is no womb. There is external growth outside of the body into a shape of a circle, from the stomach. And the seeded child, perhaps it is a good term to use, is protruding from the stomach into this sphere and the sphere is then removed and placed into a temperature regulated system, and once this is done, the body is maintained to grow for a period that is seven months on your area and the process from the sexual interaction to the body, takes one and one third of your years.

Jefferson: So, after you fertilize the women through sexual intercourse, the little thing, the fertilized "egg" stays in the women's body for how long?

Tassasol: One and one third year.

Jefferson: Okay. Then you open her body and take it out.

Tassasol: It is not opening the body because it is not directly inside of the body as they are within your race. It is externally protruding and then the excess skin is removed and the child is taken and then placed into the temperature regulated environment for a seven month period.

Jefferson: Oh! I see. So it is like she is carrying a purse in front of her belly, then you can just take the purse off and hang it somewhere else for it to grow!

Tassasol: Yes. This analogy is very sufficient.

Jefferson: So then once you take the purse off, in the other place, where do you place them?

Tassasol: It is in a temperature regulated container unit, where nutrition is given to it. And once the seven month period is over, then it is fully developed.

Jefferson: Wow. So when you place in this 'chamber'... do you put it inside water or you just take the purse and you have it on somewhere or you leave it there anywhere since it is already in the right temperature so you don't really need to put the purse inside water or anything related to the liquid idea?

Tassasol: There is no liquid but there is extra moisturized particles that are put in there to keep it in a more tempered environment... uh...

Jefferson: Humid?

Tassasol: Yes. Humid environment. Once the humidity is larger, then we are able to give food and nutrition to this growing child. We do this by directly placing the food within the external bud, and it absorbs directly through the skin.

Jefferson: Wow. So, then, once it is there, placed in this chamber, how long does it take to leave the purse?

Tassasol: Seven months.

Jefferson: Okay. So after that year that it spends with mom, then it is going, still, to spend seven months in this chamber.

Tassasol: Correct. So over all you are looking at a period, in your ideas of time, slightly close to two years in a full development from beginning to end.

Jefferson: Right. So when you say full development, because when we are born, we are born like babies, you know, really small and we still need to be carried around, to be cleaned... Is that the same with you?

Tassasol: It grows smaller than our average height of our race. Its approximately one and one half of the feet.

Jefferson: Oh, I see. Once it is "released" it can walk around, it has its eyes opened and full size hair...

Tassasol: The hair is something that grows along as does the body. But it is developed enough to walk and maintain certain controls of the body.

Jefferson: Right. Okay. So do you separate child, teenager and adulthood?

Tassasol: Yes. There are various levels of development but these are greatly depending on the individual who is growing.

Jefferson: I see. How long can you stay in your physical body?

Tassasol: For approximately 1500.

Jefferson: How old are you?

Tassasol: Specifically my age is 298.

Jefferson: Oh you are pretty young!

Tassasol: Compared to some, yes.

Jefferson: What do you look like?

Tassasol: We are about two and one half feet of your size. We are having short brownish hair. I think brown, between a brown and a black that is more sufficient. And we have very, very dark-gray skin.

Jefferson: Dark-gray skin... and what is the color of your eyes?

Tassasol: They are brown.

Jefferson: Do you get old?

Tassasol: We reach limitations of ourselves. As we get older, there is less that can be done in a physical way but its not due to physical strength. It is due... dealing more with the will and want to do certain things. As we grow older, our energetic selves are becoming "less potent". So the will to do certain things are of a lesser nature. And you see this in your race too with people who are becoming elderly. Even though the physical body is more manifested and showing its end of its cycle, internally, this is the same for all creatures. At the end of their cycles, they have done most of what they wish to do and the will to move forward is less and once the will to move forward is done no more, this is when the consciousness is released.

Jefferson: Are men and women the same?

Tassasol: They are different in some ways, but similar.

Jefferson: In what ways are they different other than the genitals?

Tassasol: Besides the genital areas... the heads of the women on our race are slightly bigger and the size of the chest area for the men is wider and there are muscular differences in the appendages, the fingers and toes.

Jefferson: Muscular differences... like... men are stronger?

Tassasol: No. Muscular in the way that the muscles are set up. There are several muscular connections within the finger, for men, which gives us more flexibility with hands, it gives us more ability to move the appendages in a quicker way.

Jefferson: Why don't women have that?

Tassasol: This is a natural thing that has happened from progression. It really affects us not now as it was when we were younger as a race. When we were finding our own food... doing things of this sort. I suppose this is a trait that stuck with us.

Jefferson: When you say progression do you mean evolution through time?

Tassasol: Yes. When you see time the way that you do, yes.

Jefferson: Alright. Do you wear clothing?

Tassasol: We have things that go around our body. I am not sure if you would call them clothing.

Jefferson: Well it is just something you wear to... for different reasons!

Tassasol: Yes. There is protective things that we wear on the body. Yes. Perhaps clothes is a word... uh...

Jefferson: Why did you say protective? What do they protect you from?

Tassasol: We wear suits that are made that have thickness. Our planet is very wet and very moist but it is made of a lot of water and a lot of ice. So it is cold and wet, and we wear this to keep ourselves more temperature regulated.

Jefferson: Wow. Okay. Do you make toilet trips?

Tassasol: Toilet trips are not used by our race.

Jefferson: Hmm. So you definitely... your body doesn't create waste.

Tassasol: No.

Jefferson: Do you kiss one another?

Tassasol: Uh... Kissing?... No.

Jefferson: Do you do anything instead, different from kissing that has the same expression?

Tassasol: There are connections of love that we show. There is touching the legs and touching the arms. And moving towards each other. Standing very close. There are many ways to show affection. But the most is with your actions that you show towards someone. If you truly have affection for them you will show them kindness and great attention to them.

Jefferson: Do you have a system of education?

Tassasol: The education system that we have is... after the specific person is born, then we put them into a system with other children where they are all able to learn from each other and also adults or grown ups coming into there and give them vibrationally, telepathically and verbally... uh... are always answering every question that they would have.

Jefferson: Do you have religion?

Tassasol: Religion is something that we don't use. We have an understanding of external entity that... I supposed you would call... the way we see it is that the one who creates the universe is also outside of this and we don't find needs to pray but we do find needs to thank, to show them gratitude for giving us the enlightenment we have to use in the way that we need to, to give us an experience that is grand and vast and eternal. Just as he is able to have the grand and vast and eternal experience. It is a gift that is given to us.

Jefferson: You said you show them gratitude. When you say them, do you mean the divine providence?

Tassasol: Them? Uh... All things that are. All specific ideas and energies in God. And manifestations of ideas of gods. We give all of it praise. Everything that is.

Jefferson: So it is almost as if you were saying that God is all in all.

Tassasol: Yes. You could see it that way. Yes. Everything that we understand is God itself. Even in the way that we try to understand that is also part of him. It is not a "him" but this is a reference for you to understand.

Jefferson: And when you say we express gratitude, it is that you live in the moment, follow your heart and by being fully who you truly are, you are then expressing gratitude for the gift of life.

Tassasol: Correct! Because we are showing that this life was not wasted. That this life was given for a reason so that we may enjoy every moment.

Jefferson: Right. Because some people may understand that when you express gratitude you gather and you sing or you kneel and you put your hands together and you say thanks, thanks, thanks three times.

Tassasol: Even in this, this is showing gratitude if this is the most exciting thing for you to do. Yes.

Jefferson: Right. But it is not like... is that the way it happens in your?... It is... It is...

Tassasol: Oh no. This is not what we would do.

Jefferson: Right, right.

Tassasol: For those who do this, the same gratitude that is shown... are just different force or different way.

Jefferson: Understood. Right. What you are saying is that everyone is free to choose however they want to express their gratitude as soon as you don't get into the trap of believing that that gratitude needs to be expressed that way.

Tassasol: I suppose even if you do believe this idea, this is sufficient as long as it is what excites you the most.

Jefferson: Right.

Tassasol: It is about what is the most exciting. If being trapped into a certain way of showing gratitude is the most exciting then this is acceptable.

Jefferson: Right. So, talking about acceptable things... let us talk about something that on Earth it is no longer as acceptable for its practices. Do you have government there?

Tassasol: Government is a difficult word. Government means many things to many differences people or entities. Because they describe ways of living in a society as government and some describe it as structured forces. But for us there is no specific interactions from one telling others what to do. In this way there is no government, but there are different people and different that are expressed to connect to other entities that reside outside of our system. There is also ones who help other ones who would look to guidance when they come to their challenges in their situations. So there are many different functions for ones who tend to serve a higher understanding than others and which they always look for to show help or guidance. But they are never told what to do. They are just given advice.

Jefferson: Are your cities the same as ours? Can you give us an idea of what your cities look like?

Tassasol: The cities that we have tend to be under the surface. We have many, many frozen areas of water on our planet and we also have open water but we keep the living areas below this in a temperature regulated setting, controlled. The surface area is very frigid and we can survive in it. It is not something that we can't. But we prefer to live under the ground.

Jefferson: Are your floors slippery?

Tassasol: No. They are quite sufficient.

Jefferson: Do you have systems of transportation?

Tassasol: Yes. We are able to move around the planet in various ways. The most specific is the universal craft which is a singular unity that can carry up to two or three people but usually it is meant for one and everyone has one of this and we are able to transport anywhere on our planet or off the planet as we choose.

Jefferson: Can you quickly say what that looks like?

Tassasol: It is just a small cylindrical... not cylindrical, this is not the right expression. It does not look like a drinking cup but it looks like one that is elongated. So it looks very long and then flattened at each end and it is very small and skinny. And the width of it is the same on all sides.

Jefferson: I see. What is your job or passion in your race and is it both one and the same?

Tassasol: Yes. The things that we do enjoy the most is what we do everyday. To me, my greatest joy comes with teaching. I love to teach others within our own race and with other people as well.

Jefferson: Do you travel outside your solar system?

Tassasol: Oh yes! Very, very often.

Jefferson: So... how?

Tassasol: In the craft, that I explained? The singular one? I can go through... I can leave the area of my planet and go to the other side either through the water or through the air and also can leave out of our planet on this.

Jefferson: Are you in the future?

Tassasol: Uh... future?... No! The time is the same.

Jefferson: Alright. How did you get this invitation?

Tassasol: Through Treb. He has sent out, maybe three weeks ago... uh... there was an intent sent out and many of us wished to connect to this intent and we all decided and thought and all of us are a part of this now. All who wish to be are here connecting now. But it was my voice that was chosen to speak.

Jefferson: Why?

Tassasol: I am not sure. Everyone has agreed.

Jefferson: Oh.

Tassasol: One moment I will ask them.

***[Silence]

Tassasol: Because they said... it was the best idea.

Jefferson: [Giggles] Alright. Uh... So we are ready to listen to what your planet has to share with ours? And I would be most excited to sit back and listen to you carefully. Thank you very much. The floor is yours.

Tassasol: Thank you. We of the Kalameelo people want to express the love that we have for you. Even though we are a race of human like beings we still look slightly different from you, in size, of appearance... but what matters is the inside of us is all on the same. This is the lesson that has not being learned yet on your planet with your race. One is easy to look at another and see the differences instead of similarities; but it is the differences that push you apart and the similarities that bring you together. You can ask how is this the same as this when nothing about it are similar? But when you look into the deeper aspects with these people, everything is similar. You have love which you are made of. You have an eternal soul which lasts forever. You have many incarnations in the separate idea of what is connected to each other for larger growth. And you also have a want and need to be who you are. So if you consider the similarities they are much greater than the differences. This can help you achieve a harmonious environment to be able to produce the greatest race that you can be. And we hope that you will take the steps that you want to take to make yourselves grow in a more connected way. Because we understand the benefits of doing so. And we hope that you take these words into your heart and find a way to make a part of your everyday existence. Thank you.

Jefferson: Excellent! How did you enjoy sharing your message on behalf of all those people?

Tassasol: Very greatly! It was a collective experience. Even though my voice is used all of their hearts and thoughts are being manifested through this conversation.

Jefferson: Wow, and how many people are there, there?

Tassasol: There are connected in a link of mind ways... uh... 12 million!

Jefferson: [Laughter] That is a lot!

Tassasol: Yes. That was all of the ones who wanted to speak.

Jefferson: [Giggles] Oh wow. So, uh... I am part of the history of 12 million people!

Tassasol: Oh and beyond! I am sure... my understanding is that you have done this with many races...

Jefferson: [Giggles] Right!

Tassasol: And if you have, you have been a part of a greater history of first communication outward.

Jefferson: Wow. So, do you guys keep an archive at all?

Tassasol: There are records that are stored, yes.

Jefferson: So how would this chat we had go into that archive?

Tassasol: It would be placed as Earth contact zero point one.

Jefferson: So this is the first time that you talk to a human being from Earth.

Tassasol: Yes and it would be one point one if it was a physical contact. And zero point one with a speaking contact and two point one if it was an intimate interchanging of densities, physical contact.

Jefferson: Wow, thank you very much for sharing that. And how are you connecting from your planet to mine? I know it is through the reptilian man, Treb Bor yit-NE, but how... how are you doing in your planet to connect to him and to me?

Tassasol: I am only sitting on my area that I choose to sit on at this timing. And I am connecting to all of the ones who wish to connect to you and we place our collective consciousness into one energy and then project this simultaneously.

Jefferson: Wow. We are running out of time, as we understand the idea of time here. I thank you very much for your presence and your energy and your knowledge. It is all very interesting. And not only that... important for us to understand the message you shared about the plurality of... not only inhabited worlds but the diversity in life experiences that helps us grow in consciousness and in spirit. So I thank you very much and I wish you to tell those 12 million people, as soon as you have the opportunity, personally, thank them. To tell them that I love them very much and I thank them for the intention to be part of this connection.

Tassasol: They all hear you now and re-express that love back to you in a way that you understand verbally as I love you as well, or I love you too.

Jefferson: Right. How do you say that in your language?

Tassasol: I am not sure if that can be translated so easily.

Jefferson: Okay so how long is that going to take you to hug each one of them?

Tassasol: Uh... hugging?... Oh! Yes. If this is the correct physical maneuvering with arms around... uh... it will probably take about 78 days.

Jefferson: Okay, will you do that?

Tassasol: Uh.. yes. If I can get 78 days of worth of a connection where all of us come together in one area, and if it is in their interest, it will be done.

Jefferson: Right. So... I was just kidding. But thank you very much and, you have yourself a wonderful life. And it was a delight to have the opportunity to connect to your race you are a very lovely people.

Tassasol: Thank you very much. And before I disconnect, I want to assure you, I understand that this is just an expression of words but I assure you, you will never run out of time! And this is the best that I can give you.

Jefferson: Fantastic! Thank you very much.

Tassasol: Good bye.

Jefferson: Good bye Tassasol!

$UNAJE JEPIL$ HUMAN$

Chapter 9
09/07/2012

Planet: KissTorNaoh
Lifespan: 220 years

Spokesperson: SunjilKajone
Age: 111 years old

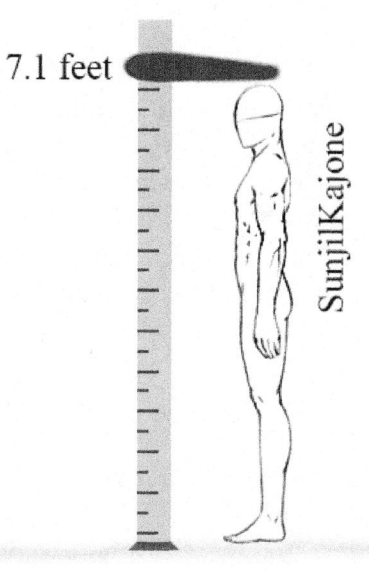

7.1 feet — SunjilKajone

Galactic Human: Hello Jefferson.

Jefferson: Hello... uh... who are you?

Galactic Human: My name is SunjilKajone

Jefferson: I understand from a previous conversation with Treb Bor yit-NE, that you are in the same density as we are, the third density.

SunjilKajone: Uh... yes. This is what Treb calls this level. Yes. Third density it is.

Jefferson: Wow. So let me start from here... in what constellation are you?

SunjilKajone: Uh... I am not sure... one moment. The sky pattern, that you have, is known to be Perseus.

***[Perseus is a constellation in the northern sky, named after the Greek hero Perseus. It was one of the 48 constellations listed by the 2nd century astronomer Ptolemy, and remains one of the 88 modern constellations defined by the International Astronomical Union. It contains the famous variable star Algol (β Per), and is also the location of the radiant of the annual Perseids meteor shower. Source: Wikipedia.]

Jefferson: Right. And what is the name of your planet?

SunjilKajone: Our planet's name is KissTorNaoh

Jefferson: And what is the size of your planet? Is it as big as ours in comparison?

SunjilKajone: Uh... size of your planet?... it is bigger! From what I understand.

Jefferson: Uh huh. How long is a day for you there?

SunjilKajone: The time period is 32 hours of yours.

Jefferson: What is the color of your skies?

SunjilKajone: The color of our skies is a light blue color.

Jefferson: How many people do you have there?

SunjilKajone: With me?

Jefferson: No, in the planet.

SunjilKajone: 194 millions.

Jefferson: Okay. And with you there, now?

SunjilKajone: There are several people, sitting and speaking to you.

Jefferson: Speaking to you?

SunjilKajone: Uh... they are hearing me speak to you as if I am channeling you.

Jefferson: [Laughter]. That is cool! [Laughter]. Wow. So, if we are coming from outside your planet, what does the planet look like?

SunjilKajone: Coming down from the top into the planet, if you are outside of the planet and looking back... if that is what you mean?

Jefferson: Yes.

SunjilKajone: If you are very far away it appears to be a very elegant and light blue color, but the closer you get the more details of our planets that you see. And you see more green and white and brown details on the surface.

Jefferson: Wow. So, what is the set up of your solar system there?

SunjilKajone: ...Solar system?... You mean the way our Sun... or star is set up?

Jefferson: Yes. With the planets.

SunjilKajone: Uh... there is one star and it is approximately the same of yours that I understand. And we have 18 planets from close to the star to the very outskirts of its gravitational hold.

Jefferson: Which planet is yours?

SunjilKajone: The fourth.

Jefferson: What is the average temperature there?

SunjilKajone: The average temperature varies. We have many different climates. We have the pole areas. How you see it to be a pole. These are both very cold. They are approximately -60 or -70 degree [Fahrenheit]. And when you get close to the middle, exact middle line that divides the planet in half. This tends to be more towards the 80 degrees area. I have an understanding that temperature settings are very, very close to yours.

Jefferson: Wow. How many moons do you have for your planet?

SunjilKajone: There are two satellites. One that is very large and one that is very small. Its is very dim to the naked eye.

Jefferson: Wow. How are you guys born?

SunjilKajone: A sexual nature. There is an interaction of sexual organs and once this is done, there is a seed that is planted... uh... very much like your sexual reproduction and then there is an elongated time of holding of the child. What is this called?

Jefferson: Pregnancy!

SunjilKajone: Yes, and this specific term is a three year long cycle of holding the child into the body. And then there is a birth of this through the same organ that you connect to have the child or to see the child and this is for the exiting of the child from the body.

Jefferson: So, how is it born then?

SunjilKajone: Through the same organ that you use to implant the seed. It is pushed through this.

Jefferson: Okay. And do you ever cut the belly?

SunjilKajone: Uh... cut the belly?... Ah, no! No. I am understanding now what you mean. No.

Jefferson: So, do you separate childhood from teenager, from adulthood?

SunjilKajone: There are various degrees of growth. When you have a child and they are newly born, they are fairly ignorant of facts, ignorant of the ways of society at least with a verbal and physical way, they are not ignorant in an energy connection way, they are actually more adapted to this than most of the older ones. But they are ignorant of the physical knowledge. And once they grow, there is more moving of the body and more moving of the words. And this growth is very simple and last for seven years, until it is more understanding of the ways, more intimate in knowledge and more intimate in the physical aspects. And once this happens, then they go through a growing period until they are fully developed. And once they are fully developed, then they become much older until their body no longer gives them the same degree of energy that it needs. And then we become very old and die. And this whole process from beginning to end, takes approximately 220 years.

Jefferson: So... that... that was my question, how long can you stay in your physical body? Is that 220 years?

SunjilKajone: Yes, from the time we are born. This is an average, of course. There is not one specific number but there are many ages that we are able to leave the body.

Jefferson: And do you definitely then, as you said, you do get old.

SunjilKajone: Yes. There is a physical aging that appears. Much as most of our level of consciousness, to my understanding.

Jefferson: How old are you, yourself?

SunjilKajone: I am personally, 111.

Jefferson: What do you look like?

SunjilKajone: Uh... compared to your race, that I understand, we are slightly taller. Around 7 feet tall. We have much hair on the face and slightly more on our body than some of you do. I understand that some of your ethnicities are hairy. So we are fairly having more hair growing in all of us. And the facial hair for the men is much, much more than it would be for female. Our faces have very similar structures with nose and the chicks and the mouth shape in very similar ways. As well as the ears, and the necks. And our bodies are slightly elongated, compared to yours.

Jefferson: How tall are you?

SunjilKajone: I am about 7.1 feet.

Jefferson: What is the color of your eyes?

SunjilKajone: It is green.

Jefferson: Is that for everybody?

SunjilKajone: No. There is green, there is purple, there is orange, there is blue, there is red...

Jefferson: That is nice. I never heard of a third density race with orange and purple eyes. Well, then I haven't heard much from other races, but that is interesting.

SunjilKajone: Yes. There are many looks to our people. I understand you have a diversity of skin color.

Jefferson: Right.

SunjilKajone: And hair types. Our skin colors are to a lesser degree than yours. Uh... but we still have differences in coloring of skins.

Jefferson: What is the color of your skin?

SunjilKajone: For me, myself, is approximately what you would see, a man of Portuguese descent.

Jefferson: I see, lets say a number, from black to white. White being 100 and black being 0.

SunjilKajone: For me within myself?

Jefferson: Yeah.

SunjilKajone: This would be... you are saying 100 is white and 0 is black?

Jefferson: Yeah.

SunjilKajone: It would be a 24, 25.

Jefferson: Oh I see, so you are darker than you are white.

SunjilKajone: Yes.

Jefferson: And uh... but what is the... what is the one that gets closer to 100 in your race, in skin color?

SunjilKajone: Well there... we do not divide our race into skin colors because this is something we have no true need for so there are no specific areas within our planet that has only these colors. It is very, very wide. There are many who have closer to 100. And there are many that are around this area, plus on the other side of the planet.

Jefferson: Right. Yeah. Yeah. No, I was just wondering if you had people that are... I was wondering how close to white people in your world can get. That was my question.

SunjilKajone: Oh, yes. Yes! If 100 is the purest white color with no variations, than the closest our race would be, would be 65.

Jefferson: I see. Yes. That is pretty much what I wanted to know. Alright. So, are men and women the same? Do they look the same?

SunjilKajone: No. Our females have larger chest areas and larger leg, the upper legs. And they also have less hair on the face and on the body.

Jefferson: Right. So, do they have hairs on the top of the head?

SunjilKajone: Oh yes. We all have hair that resides strictly on the back and top portions of our head, some on the sides of our head.

Jefferson: How long down does it go?

SunjilKajone: It is preference for everyone. For me specifically, it is coming to the middle of my... uh... about my area that you would call a butt.

Jefferson: Okay. So you have to have haircuts every once in a while.

SunjilKajone: If we wish to have them, yes.

Jefferson: Do you wear clothing?

SunjilKajone: Yes. We wear clothing... each one of our clothing is different. But for me specifically, I wear something that resembles... uh... what your race would call a cloak or a coat. It is very long and it has two leggings that comes to the waist and then a top half that is open in the arms and is put around the stomach and a hole for the head. And you can also take the back of the area of the clothing and place it over your head for rain or for other weather that is not tailorable.

Jefferson: Oh I see. Do you have to make toilet trips?

SunjilKajone: Toilet trips?... Oh... excretions of waste?

Jefferson: Yes.

SunjilKajone: Yes. There are those times where we must release what we are not using.

Jefferson: Right so you go for both. You go for number 1 and number 2.

SunjilKajone: Number 1 and 2?... Oh! No. There is an excretion of liquid, only.

Jefferson: Oh. I see. And it is the same as us, through your genital organ?

SunjilKajone: Yes, it is in the same location. But for your, there is... it is not the same, directly inwardly and the mechanics of it, but yes, in the same general genital area.

Jefferson: Do you kiss one another?

SunjilKajone: Kiss?... Uh... No! There is no kissing.

Jefferson: How do you show affection?

SunjilKajone: A holding of hands towards each other. And also an embracing where you are standing next to someone and placing your palm of the hand in the upper or lower back or upper butt area.

Jefferson: How does education work in your planet?

SunjilKajone: For us to be taught of the way... we are given opportunities once the age comes where you are able to absorb more information, then you stay with your family and I understand some parts of your world have what you call extended families, where it is all of the family members, all brothers and sisters, children, aunts, uncles, all of those types of relations, they live in no one specific designated area. And we have some of this in some parts of the world. And where we are from we place the children within the family structures who are there, able to obtain all the knowledge that they are able to give. And then if there is something that none of us understands or are able to teach, then we will find ones who are in our local areas and communities.

Jefferson: Wow. Are you are type 1, type 2 or type 3 civilization? Let me explain, I don't think you know what I am talking about. Right?

SunjilKajone: Correct.

Jefferson: Let me tell you. There is a theoretical physicist in our planet who divided the civilizations into type 1, 2 and 3. I'll give you a quick intro:

Type one: This civilization harnesses the energy output of an entire planet.
Type two: This civilization harnesses the energy of a star and generates about ten billion times the energy output of a type one civilization.
And Type three: This civilization harnesses the energy output of a galaxy. About then billion times the energy output of a

type two civilization.

So, for instance... hey write down so that you can answer later yes?...

Type one civilization: Would be able to manipulate, truly, planetary energies. They might for example, control or modify the weather. They would have the power to manipulate planetary phenomena such as hurricanes which can release the energy of hundreds of hydrogen bombs, perhaps volcano or even earth quakes may be altered by such civilization. Let us talk about this type one civilization, is that the one you are already? We are not even type one. We are zero!

SunjilKajone: Yes, we are nothing capable of producing those types of catastrophes I suppose. Is the best word to describe them. We are able to do nothing of those magnitude.

Jefferson: So you are not able to manipulate planetary phenomena.

SunjilKajone: No.

Jefferson: So as to use the energy of the hurricanes or the volcano...

SunjilKajone: A volcano is one that produces hot things.

Jefferson: Lava.

SunjilKajone: We are not able to make one of these work but we are able to use ones in existence for heat energy.

Jefferson: Right. So you can definitely use the powers of nature to progress your society.

SunjilKajone: In ways, yes. With those, yes. Hurricanes, tornados, no. Uh... These things do not exist. Our weather system does not allow this.

Jefferson: Oh.

SunjilKajone: There are much rain and electricity. At the electric level of electricity, we are able to harness much of this and use it within our society.

Jefferson: So, a type two civilization might be able to manipulate the power of solar flares for instance. They can harness the energy of a star. So are you type one, type two, or type three do you think?

SunjilKajone: If we have to have a choice between all three, it would be more towards a type one. We are able to use Sun mechanisms. The sun that comes down to our planet. We are able to use the heat and light generated from this to create some energy. But not in a direct manner such as a solar flare being used specifically to do things with.

Jefferson: By contrast we are a type zero civilization which extracts its energy from dead plants, oil and coal. Did you know that?

SunjilKajone: Uh... coal?... oh no. Yes. Our early civilization used similar techniques. The burning of plants and also deposits of carbon to fuel, steamed generated mechanisms. But this was in our early development.

Jefferson: Are you more evolved spiritually than we are on

Earth?

SunjilKajone: Uh... if you compare collective consciousnesses, uh... I would understand us to be slightly more progressed than yours. We do not have murderings, or the rapings or the violence towards each other. There are altercation and upsetting in the raising of the energies in negative ways, sometimes, but there is not the level of your race's capabilities of expressing those angry feelings in a violent way. So, perhaps slightly more.

Jefferson: Do you have religion?

SunjilKajone: Religious ideas?... Uh... we all have our own individual understandings of what God is but there is no organizing setting for it.

Jefferson: What is the meaning of life for you?

SunjilKajone: To grow, to take care of the ones that we love and for us, as a family to help other families and to help everyone that we can as often as we can. As they will help us. The meaning is to grow and to love and to do as much as you can to grow as a whole of society. And this has been a very, very strong mindset and instilled, not only for our family but many families around our planet.

Jefferson: And do you have pets?

SunjilKajone: Pets... Oh! Animals? Yes. We have many animals, we do not enclose them into cages. That is not very nice to the animal.

Jefferson: I know.

SunjilKajone: So they run free and we interact with many of them. There are many that have progressed to a level where we don't need to enclose them, they come to us now, similar thinking to the domesticated animals that you have such as dogs, and cats and horses... where they are naturally interacting with us now because of the time that we have spent with them in earlier parts of our civilizations.

Jefferson: Can you share one example?

SunjilKajone: There is an animal that has four legs that stands to be 5 feet. It has a very broad chest and stomach area. It has a very long what is the letter? S... "S"-shaped neck, a sort of curved neck, and his head is very round and its eyes are three quarters the size of its head. And it has a small mouth and a long nose and it has two protruding extensions on the top of the head, with large balls on each one of them and those are called a... Adana. And those are very friendly to us.

Jefferson: Okay. So, is it. In any way close to the horses that we have idea?

SunjilKajone: Hmm. The legs are not the same. The neck is not the same; their head is not the same.

Jefferson: Right.

SunjilKajone: But perhaps the body shape, the chest and stomach area, but more rounded.

Jefferson: Oh okay. What is that for? What do you use that for?

SunjilKajone: Use what for?

Jefferson: This creature?

SunjilKajone: Oh we do not use them for anything. They come to us and interact with us.

Jefferson: Okay. So it just makes you happy to have them.

SunjilKajone: Oh yes. To interact and to connect to them is very exciting for many of us.

Jefferson: And do you have what we call cats?

SunjilKajone: No.

Jefferson: Oh... any furry creatures like cats?

SunjilKajone: Uh... the Adana does have a slight fur to it, very fluffy. But as for smaller animals there is no fluff, fluffy ones. There are ones that have skin that have small hairs on it, the likeness of a rabbit but not with the ears and these are shaped differently.

Jefferson: What is the color of that animal you just spoke of, before this one.

SunjilKajone: Oh the Adana?

Jefferson: Yes.

SunjilKajone: There are multiple colors but mostly in a green and mostly in a red and mostly in an orange.

Jefferson: And what is the color of the eyes?

SunjilKajone: It varies as well, it can be blue, it can be...

Jefferson: Oh you know what? I think it makes it easier you to send me a picture of it.

SunjilKajone: Uh... if you close your eyes I will send you one now.

Jefferson: Ah... but in our planet it is not easy to do those transfers and downloads. I know for you it seems easy, I tell you close your eyes and I will send you but for us, when we close our eyes, we imagine stuff. We never know if we are making it up or imagining the real deal. You know? So I mean, send me a picture then... like through the intergalactic postal services!

SunjilKajone: Oh, now I understand what you mean.

Jefferson: Yes.

SunjilKajone: Yes. I am not sure if they come this way.

Jefferson: Okay, well, we will see if we can work that out with Treb, okay?

SunjilKajone: Yes.

Jefferson: Do you take pictures there?

SunjilKajone: Uh... not in the sense that you do.

Jefferson: Yeah but you know how to draw.

SunjilKajone: Yes there are ones who do draw, there are ones who do make more detailed accounts of physical things, yes.

Jefferson: Yes. So, who is the best? The best guy that does that?

SunjilKajone: There are many that are best. They all have separate individual style or variations of the same. As for ones that look very real. There are many, if they are doing it, they are loving to do it and they are good at it. So all who like to draw are good at doing so.

Jefferson: Okay, so will you tell one of them to have one drawn and then you figure out with Treb about how to make it get to my place.

SunjilKajone: Uh... I can speak to him about this and see what he wished to do.

Jefferson: Okay. We do that perhaps towards the end. Let me follow up with other questions. How do you see God?

SunjilKajone: For me it is a personal connection and a feeling. When I feel joy and happiness, this is more parts of a God. When I feel sorrow or pain or suffering of the heart. This is also God, but in a lesser form. There are many ways to experience and they are all within the actions and feelings that you have.

Jefferson: Do you have government?

SunjilKajone: Government?... uh... no! Not a structure of government. We have many people who are in charge of many different things. But they are all helped and they do not make decisions based on their own needs but of all needs.

Jefferson: Right! That is what we need: enlightened scientists in strategic places taking care to direct the resources of our planet and applying leading edge knowledge towards social concern!

SunjilKajone: Yes! That is a brilliant aspect!

Jefferson: That is how you work, right?

SunjilKajone: Perhaps not scientists at all places. But yes, ones who have an understanding of what they are doing, yes.

Jefferson: Right. Are your cities the same as ours?

SunjilKajone: No. We have very simple structures that are made from natural occurrences.

Jefferson: Oh.

SunjilKajone: Like if you see a rock protruding.

Jefferson: A cave.

SunjilKajone: Uh... similar, but we make them as our own and we take out of the rock so we are carving them inside the sides of wall. What your plateaus perhaps, or... caves is another way to see it. But an inward rock dwelling.

Jefferson: And also houses on the trees...

SunjilKajone: Yes, there are some breed of trees that grow very large and have wide spans and there are many who dwell there as well.

Jefferson: And in the oceans?

SunjilKajone: Not as many but there are ones who make crafts and live out into the oceans.

Jefferson: [Laughter] Wow. Do you have system of transportation?

SunjilKajone: Yes. Water related... uh... driving in a, what you would think of to be a, sound wave technology. And this is how all of our technology is built. This allows us to have a water craft.... this allows us to have crafts that go back and forth to each area of our planet. As you would see a car, almost. It has wheels and its propulsion is taken care by the sound vibration and it goes to anywhere that you wish to go. There are also ones that fly and there are ones that fly longer distances.

Jefferson: What is your job and what is your passion in your race or are both one and the same?

SunjilKajone: For me? As a specific nature, I am much of what you would think of a channeler. One who connects to other entities and translates these ideas to our people. One who is able to connect energies perhaps slightly better than the rest of the ones who are around me or slightly more in my interest to do so than the ones who are not.

Jefferson: Do you travel outside your planet?

SunjilKajone: Uh... there are distances that are short but yes, we have made to several other planets within our system.

Jefferson: Do you travel outside your solar system?

SunjilKajone: This is not done yet. This is something that we continue to progress on. The further we are going, the more we see our capabilities to do so.

Jefferson: Have you visited just your moons or other planets around?

SunjilKajone: Four other planets that we have. One before us, on the third planet and three outside the fifth. The sixth and the seventh.

Jefferson: Right. Are you in the future?

SunjilKajone: The future?... No! We share your time.

Jefferson: Okay. So we are ready to hear your message. Are you ready to share it with us?

SunjilKajone: Yes. It would be great to share. I want to tell you all that once you understand your own inside, this can become a great tool to use. When you connect to others and do not understand them and do not see them in the light that they are deserving to be seen at, as an equal to you and as one who is made of spirit and one that is made of love, than you lessen the own means of seeing yourself. When you connect to everyone, they are the same as you. But you must see the small and petty differences and remove them. Our society in a recent history has had many ups and downs. Not so much struggling with each other but struggling with ourselves. And this is where all struggle begins. Within yourself. So when you see everything around you as faulted, it isn't because your world is faulted. It is because you are not able to see yourself in a light that is not faulted. And I hope that you are able to use this lesson in the everyday situation to help yourselves so that you may help others. Thank you.

Jefferson: Fantastic. Thank you very much. Did you enjoy sharing that message with us?

SunjilKajone: Yes, very much.

Jefferson: How did you get this invitation to speak to me?

SunjilKajone: From the one that you call Treb.

Jefferson: Right. But how?

SunjilKajone: During one of the connections that I was making. I felt an energy coming in and the energy I connected to was more than happy to relinquish itself for one moment so that Treb could come in.

Jefferson: Uh huh.

SunjilKajone: And when he comes in, he asks the person who speaks and asks questions and thoughts and mindsets being passed. He asked if it was acceptable and I communicated and told him it was acceptable to do so. So now we made this connection later.

Jefferson: So, how are you connecting? Do you just close your eyes? Do you need any help, assistance from technology?

SunjilKajone: No. If I close my eyes and close my mouth I am able to feel this energy. And once the energy comes into me I am able to translate the waves of energy into words.

Jefferson: So basically how many people do you have around you right now?

SunjilKajone: Several hundred.

Jefferson: And they are all listening to me.

SunjilKajone: Yes.

Jefferson: Because you are translating the thoughts that you are getting from the channeler here and then from the reptilian Treb.

SunjilKajone: And from you as well. The conversation that you and I are having, they are hearing. As well as interpretations and ideas from the one you call Treb.

Jefferson: I see. Okay. So... did you call everyone, did they come by hazard... how come you are all united there, together... Was it purposefully for this meeting?

SunjilKajone: There was an understanding that the connection would be made at this specific time. And all of the ones here were interested to see what it was going to be. There are many informations that are exchanged. But this one specifically through the specific ones here.

Jefferson: Uh huh. Does anybody know Earth? Is there a particular excitement about our planet?

SunjilKajone: Several here do have an understanding of Earth, of what it is and who the earthlings are. Yes.

Jefferson: Do you want to ask the most excited one to... if they have any questions that I might... just one that I might... perhaps help with?

SunjilKajone: Uh... one moment as I ask.

Jefferson: Right.

SunjilKajone: One asks... is it true that people take substances to take them outside of their own feeling of consciousness to avoid dealing with the energetic suggestions... or not suggestions... energetic obstacles of growing? And they take these substances in various ways, such as placing in the mouth or placing in mechanisms to put within their bodies to make them feel outside of themselves? I believe they are speaking of, what you refer to as drugs.

Jefferson: It is true, yes, that they take it. It is truth that that is one of the reason. But there are many reasons. Basically, I think that when someone is up to speed with a better reality and the external world just don't allow them to express the entirety of themselves, they might turn back in and enclose themselves with those ideas that will "jump stages", so to speak, that will take them to where they "belong" so to speak. So that in that they can be who they truly are without actually, perhaps, harming others or demanding others to change so that they can be up to speed with the world that they want to live. That is also one of the reasons. And the only reason why I see it is reasonable for someone to think of going that way. But unfortunately they do not only take those ideas to have this experience, transcendence, transcendent experience, but they also... uh... exposing themselves to their weaknesses they end up getting addicted and that is destructive. So, yes. They do take it. It is for various reasons and it is unfortunate that some expose themselves to their weaknesses without knowing so and they go down a path, they find very difficult to get out of.

SunjilKajone: Thank you very much. The thanks is coming not only from the one who asked but from many.

Jefferson: What is his name? The name of the one who asked?

SunjilKajone: The one who asked name's is KahjilNamsiri.

Jefferson: So tell him I thank you very much for the interest in my planet, on our people and hope to see you guys as soon as we are out of this quarantine, as soon as it is possible, or perhaps in spirit at some point.

SunjilKajone: Yes. The thanks is given back also by everyone here.

Jefferson: Right. Much love to you and yeah... now as we disconnect I will talk to Treb and if you want to listen to our conversation, we will see about the idea of the drawing.

SunjilKajone: Yes. Thank you again.

Jefferson: Thanks.

***[Silence]

Treb Bor yit-NE: Uh... Jefferson?

Jefferson: Hey Treb Bor yit-NE.

Treb Bor yit-NE: Yes.

Jefferson: So, Treb, it came up the idea, as we were following our highest excitement that it would be interesting to see what that animal looks like that they could make a drawing and have it sent to us. And... Pleenaki already came here and... I know... and he said he was going to leave a drawing on my wall... How do you think you can facilitate the idea of this race to have the drawing to be sent to me?

Treb Bor yit-NE: As for me, as an individual, it is not of my belief system to do a physical connection. But perhaps if you are able to speak to the one... Pleenaki, perhaps he would be able to facilitate this in a way. This is not against his beliefs and he is accepting the ideas of being able to enter the planet and the atmosphere and to connect to you in this way. So perhaps it would be a better idea for him to connect with this idea and if he wishes to do this, I will make an expression of to where they are and their area of the galaxy and also what area of time they are in.

Jefferson: Alright. Thanks. Now just to make sure about his location, where did he say exactly he was from?

Treb Bor yit-NE: The one known as Perseus. There is a star, within this area that you would know to be Algol. This is a very small star, located to the west slightly, within less than one inch if you are placing a ruler to the sky, west and north of this. I am not sure what is the name of the star that your race would use but in your pattern of sky, from Earth, this is where it would be.

Jefferson: Wow. Okay, Treb. So, you said it is not in your nature and belief system the idea of physical interaction in the sense of leaving a drawing here, for instance.

Treb Bor yit-NE: Yes.

Jefferson: Is that because Pleenaki is part of civilization that doesn't respect the others?

Treb Bor yit-NE: For me the idea that you have between other races, there is a very fine line to draw. Pleenaki does not wish to interfere with you and in his belief system, coming through the atmosphere is not interference. It is one that is acceptable for their race but for my race, this is not acceptable. It is not acceptable idea because there are interactions of energy in a consistent rate, even if it is only slightly. So, for me the idea of going past many individuals, many molecules of air, water and electricity and also many plants and animal, I am therefore vibrationally interrupting very many first, very large amount of second and a very few amount of some third density entities, when I am coming through the area. So for us it is a different idea.

Jefferson: Alright. Thank you.

Treb Bor yit-NE: And this is all that you have?

Jefferson: Yes, sir!

Treb Bor yit-NE: Yes. With this been said, I will leave you this morning in love and light, and we will speak to each other, very soon.

Jefferson: Thanks.

Treb Bor yit-NE: Good bye.

Jefferson: Bye.

$OLEPION$ HUMAN$

Chapter 10
09/07/2012

Planet: SolePions
Lifespan: 3000 years

Spokesperson:
KwheelTravRiupaus
Age: 1339 years old

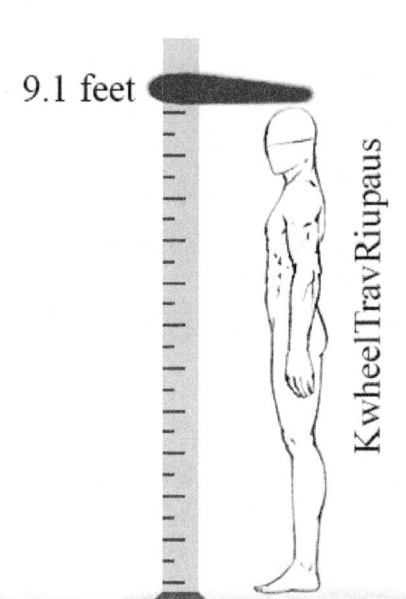

9.1 feet

KwheelTravRiupaus

Galactic Human: Greetings to you!

Jefferson: Hey! What is your name sir?

Galactic Human: My name is KwheelTravRiupaus.

Jefferson: So Treb just told me you are very excited to talk to us, why is that?

KwheelTravRiupaus: It is a very interesting time for us to speak onto each other.

Jefferson: In what sense?

KwheelTravRiupaus: Very many aspects of this. Specially the idea of becoming directly connected to your kind.

Jefferson: Whoa! Great. So what constellation are you?

KwheelTravRiupaus: One moment as I confirm.

Jefferson: Okay.

KwheelTravRiupaus: This is a Leporis area.

Jefferson: Okay. What planet are you?

KwheelTravRiupaus: The name of our planet is called the SolePions

Jefferson: What is the size of your planet? Is that as big as ours?

KwheelTravRiupaus: Approximately one and nine tenths. Almost twice.

Jefferson: Okay. How long is a day for you there?

KwheelTravRiupaus: Approximately two thirds of yours.

Jefferson: What is the color of your skies?

KwheelTravRiupaus: It is gray.

Jefferson: Wow. How many people do you have?

KwheelTravRiupaus: Close to 300 millions.

Jefferson: Okay. If you are coming from outside, what is the color of your planet?

KwheelTravRiupaus: It appears to be a white and gray.

Jefferson: Hmm. What is the solar system set up for you?

KwheelTravRiupaus: Set up in each way?

Jefferson: Like, you have how many Suns and you have how many planets... do you have moons?

KwheelTravRiupaus: Oh yes. I understand what you mean. We are a double, binary system. One which has four stars that are gravitationally linked. Two pairs of two stars that exchange gravitational combinations to make them all share one area of gravitation. And within this we are on one binary pair.
    There are ones that are slightly larger. Approximately three times of your star. And then the other binary pair are close to the same size of your star. And we are encompassing the one that is similar to your size star. There are the two stars and around both of these stars is eighteen planets but only five that are habitable.

Jefferson: And which one is yours?

KwheelTravRiupaus: We are approximately at the seventh.

Jefferson: I see. What density are you?

KwheelTravRiupaus: We reside within the fourth density from the way that you understand densities.

Jefferson: How many moons do you have around your planet?

KwheelTravRiupaus: We have no moons.

Jefferson: So do you have oceans or water bodies?

KwheelTravRiupaus: Yes. Very much water within our area. There are only small places of land. And a very thick atmosphere.

Jefferson: And do you live in the water then?

KwheelTravRiupaus: No. We do not live directly in the water.

Jefferson: Above?

KwheelTravRiupaus: On the land areas.

Jefferson: Oh. Okay. How are you guys born?

KwheelTravRiupaus: In the same way that most human races are. There are mixing of genetics into a singular physical body and this body is meant to grow.

Jefferson: So it is not from a sexual relationship from male and female?

KwheelTravRiupaus: There are genetics from both. Yes. But there is not a sexual production.

Jefferson: So is it like producing a clone?

KwheelTravRiupaus: Not in the same way because this is a singular physical structure, and for a clone you have several but they are the same. These are all individually made from genetics of one and the other and put together to form one new body.

Jefferson: Oh. Right. So the "scientists" take care of doing that.

KwheelTravRiupaus: Yes. It is similar to your scientists.

Jefferson: Alright. Do you have what we call childhood and then teenager and then adulthood?

KwheelTravRiupaus: There are only two phases that we see. And this is from birth to a full grown and from fully grown into the rest of the inner consciousness.

Jefferson: How long does it take to get to the fully grown stage?

KwheelTravRiupaus: From a physical body it takes approximately two fifty of your years.

Jefferson: Two fifty... Two hundred and fifty?

KwheelTravRiupaus: Correct.

Jefferson: Oh. And then how long can you stay in your physical body?

KwheelTravRiupaus: Perhaps 3000 or close to this.

Jefferson: And how old are you?

KwheelTravRiupaus: 1339.

Jefferson: Oh, so you are about my age!

KwheelTravRiupaus: Uh...

Jefferson: Like... I mean a third... a third to the end.

KwheelTravRiupaus: Yes, a little further than this but correct.

Jefferson: Right. So, what do you look like?

KwheelTravRiupaus: We are close to eight and one half feet as a race, this is the average. For me this is nine feet and one inch. And we are of a very dark skin with very light hair.

Jefferson: Wow.

KwheelTravRiupaus: And we share characteristics of eye color, either being a brown, a light brown or a black.

Jefferson: Do you get old?

KwheelTravRiupaus: Old?... as in a physical or as far as consciousness?

Jefferson: Physically!

KwheelTravRiupaus: Physically is not... a result of the dying cells or the dropping of consciousness followed by the body degradations; we do not have this.

Jefferson: So you look the same from year 251 to year 3000.

KwheelTravRiupaus: Aspects change in a physical way. But not in a degrading way.

Jefferson: Oh. Do they change for better?

KwheelTravRiupaus: They change as we change. It is not a drastic change but small areas. Perhaps a growth of the neck area, specific characteristics of the face are changing. And even legs changing in length at some point, very slightly.

Jefferson: Ah. What is the color of your hair?

KwheelTravRiupaus: It is what you would think to be blond.

Jefferson: That is cool! From zero being pitch back and one hundred being white, what is the color of your skin? I know you said it is dark but...

KwheelTravRiupaus: It is approximately 73, 77. This would be the darker.

Jefferson: Oh, so you are white man!

KwheelTravRiupaus: Hmm. Oh and 0? So we are reversing this!

Jefferson: Oh okay.

KwheelTravRiupaus: If black were 100, then it would be it.

Jefferson: Okay. Understood. So you are around 27. Alright. Are men and women the same?

KwheelTravRiupaus: Yes. We are very similar in looks, there are slight differences. But most cannot see with their eyes. Only by energetic means.

Jefferson: Do you wear clothing?

KwheelTravRiupaus: Protective equipment, is this what you mean?

Jefferson: Yeah.

KwheelTravRiupaus: Yes. There are layers of equipments that have us within temperature variations.

Jefferson: What is the average temperature of your planet?

KwheelTravRiupaus: In the temperatures that you have, perhaps it is closer to 75, or 80.

Jefferson: Wow. And in the case of your human physical body, do you need to go to toilet trips?

KwheelTravRiupaus: No.

Jefferson: Okay. So, you don't produce waste of any kind.

KwheelTravRiupaus: There is energetic releases from our consciousness. Energy that no longer is needed for us. If we are overcoming energetic obstacles or obstacles of a physical nature, energy is released and this is a release of some sort. It is not a waste, but it is a release of the energies we no longer need at them moment.

Jefferson: Do you kiss one another?

KwheelTravRiupaus: No.

Jefferson: How do you express your affection towards a beloved one?

KwheelTravRiupaus: With a thought intent. A thought projection.

Jefferson: Wow. How does it work for your race, the process of education.

KwheelTravRiupaus: Education is one that is of a nature... uh... perhaps not as strict as your race would see but strict for many other races in the fourth density, where you are set to learn... once your physical body is ready to be moved you are set in a series of teachings and these teachings are various. If this teaching does not resonate with you, you are able to change the course of learning in which you choose, but you must go through all of the learning process so that we all have a same understanding of all knowledge.

Jefferson: So this is from age... like... 30 to 250?

KwheelTravRiupaus: 25, yes. To 200!

Jefferson: Okay. Do you have religion?

KwheelTravRiupaus: No, there is no specific deity that we praise.

Jefferson: What is the meaning of life for you?

KwheelTravRiupaus: To do as we can to promote happiness and excitement within our own race and with other races as well. To try to become part of a larger society and to integrate ourselves with all consciousnesses.

Jefferson: Is that for the reason promoting or progressing the spiritual development of your soul?

KwheelTravRiupaus: Yes, for our soul, our race and all races that we communicate with. For everything.

Jefferson: Alright. How do you see God?

KwheelTravRiupaus: We do not see God. We do not understand a God. We understand that everything that is in creation is a part of everything that we are. So there is no specific need for an understanding of this. There is just an understanding of the way we fit into this.

Jefferson: But when you look into the idea of... say for instance, a prime creator. Do you see it as the first cause of everything and supreme intelligence?

KwheelTravRiupaus: Uh... perhaps, this is the way you can see this.

Jefferson: Right. Okay! How do you guys relate to music?

KwheelTravRiupaus: Music is not something that is done in our race. Most of the time there are ones who enjoy the vibrational changes of sound waves. But it is not very common within our people.

Jefferson: Do you have systems of government?

KwheelTravRiupaus: We have systems of... uh... how would you classify this? We have systems of learning, we have systems of production, of society and needs. We also have systems of communication. There are separate entities that reside within our planet of a specific function. But none of them is to control or overlook the race as a whole. It is only to do the jobs that we wish to do and to do it in the best way that we can. And there is no one specific person who runs each area. It is a communal understanding and agreement.

Jefferson: Do you also have your technology to assist you in those tasks?

KwheelTravRiupaus: Oh, yes. Quite definitely. We have to use more technology as our consciousness is grown. Because the ones that we have had, 20.000 years ago are not the same of what we use now. And it encompasses our larger consciousness quite well.

Jefferson: Wow. In that I would suppose your cities are not the same as ours.

KwheelTravRiupaus: No. We have no cities.

Jefferson: So, basically you sleep... where?

KwheelTravRiupaus: We do not sleep.

Jefferson: Oh. So basically when it rains, where do you hide yourself?

KwheelTravRiupaus: It is raining most of the time. Our atmosphere is very thick but this is something that our race prefers. There is no need to sleep or rest. We live directly off of the land area and we also have crafts that we use. Large crafts that can take our civilization outside of our planet to visit other places but also to facilitate technological uses.

Jefferson: Hmm. So you don't have buildings or houses or...

stuff like that?

KwheelTravRiupaus: No. We live on these land areas where there is no need for structures whatsoever. The only time we need a place to set is during the birthing process and this is located in the large ships.

Jefferson: Do you have systems of transportation? Of course, right? You have the ships and... uh... but on the floor.

KwheelTravRiupaus: There is no need for transportation, our consciousness projects us very well.

Jefferson: Okay. What is your job, or passion in your race and are both one and the same?

KwheelTravRiupaus: Yes. It is quite the same. I am one of the junior representatives of communicating to the outside world and entities.

Jefferson: Wow.

KwheelTravRiupaus: And there are many here who are doing this much longer than I am.

Jefferson: Senior!

KwheelTravRiupaus: Yes, senior. And instructors, if you will, or senior representatives of this job, yes.

Jefferson: Do you guys travel outside of your planet to other planets?

KwheelTravRiupaus: Yes. Quite often.

Jefferson: Do you travel outside of your solar system?

KwheelTravRiupaus: Yes, quite often!

Jefferson: Wow. Why is it that you go outside quite often? Because apparently your planet is unique in the sense that it is raining all the time, you don't sleep, the atmosphere is thick...

KwheelTravRiupaus: Yes, but we also must do the communication with other races so that we are able to facilitate more integration into a larger society. And because I have chosen to do this, this leads me off of the planet more than I am on the planet. But there are many who reside there, most of the time. And they are joyous to do the job in which they are doing at each time.

Jefferson: Do you have little animals like pets or... that you have in your planet?

KwheelTravRiupaus: There are no other species but ours here.

Jefferson: Wow. Alright, so... are you in the future?

KwheelTravRiupaus: If you see the time linearly, and you are saying it on a perspective of energy that is not the same as yours, so a time line in which is different, than you would see us: 1600 on a varying energy.

Jefferson: How did you get this invitation?

KwheelTravRiupaus: Communications were there and there was an entity that was called Kroyzep and he wished to express that this entity that you call Treb was looking for human type entity.

Jefferson: Kroyzep? I've spoken to him. He is very nice.

***[Kroyzep from Zanetly, was the third galactic human we spoke to in this book series].

KwheelTravRiupaus: Yes. It is a telepathic communication that I use with him, as one of the newer contacts of the entities. And in this communication this invitation was given from them to us. And so I reached out for the one who is called Treb by you, and he facilitates this communication.

Jefferson: So do you like Kroyzep's race? What do you like most about them, since they are different?

KwheelTravRiupaus: We have not have great communications. This is one that is new. I have not had a change to visit them physically.

Jefferson: Oh I see. Okay. So, how are you connecting to me right now, do you have your eyes closed, are you waking, are you under water... are you...

KwheelTravRiupaus: Right now I am on a craft and I am sitting on a sit that projects consciousness further and this helps me facilitate the connection that I have with you.

Jefferson: Oh, so you have the help of technology then.

KwheelTravRiupaus: Correct.

Jefferson: Alright. So, are you ready to share with us your message today?

KwheelTravRiupaus: Yes. I would be greatly excited.

Jefferson: Okay. So please go ahead, I will sit back and listen!

KwheelTravRiupaus: Greetings. I wish to express my understanding of your planet. It has become more in the recent time than I have had a chance to understand your race, from times before. And in the learning of your race, there are many things that are found that are building block areas of your race, in a technological sense. You are using fuels, you are using live plants and you are using nuclear energies. And these three are one of the worst ways to run your machinery. This is a very hard on the planet that is called Earth. It is one that is very devastating to your environments of mother Earth. So I wish to express to you gratitude for a collective shift, in trying to find more sustainable ways so that you are not devastating the consciousness that holds you and gives you life.

This Earth, as you call it, is a very gentle being. It is one who is in a non-physical area of consciousness that gives all of itself to you physically so that you are able to sustain your life. So in thinking of new ways to progress within your energy, try to remind yourselves that, as she gives you new life, when you use these old ways of technological advancement you are hurting her life. Continue to find the balance that is not so hard on your "mother". Try to find ways that are not going to hurt you and your race. Be it atomic, and nuclear progression that you made on your planet. You are now starting to see the effects on the planet that these have given. You are a capable race, one of great intelligence and one of great heart. If you wish to choose this portion of your own self to use in its growth, try to use this intellect and heart trying to find better ways. There are many great ways to produce sounds that will help you technologically. This is a very clean and free way to do many of the things that you wish to do. I cannot speak in details of this, because it is not willing to be facilitated the communication through the one in which I speak. The one that you call Treb, does not wish for me to further these ideas. But only in expressing the fact and ideas that this is not a judgment towards your race. Only an understanding. One that you already have of what these things are doing to the facilitating planet. So please try to understand that as you grow as you begin to think of new ways to leave your heart open, not only your mind. Your heart will further yourselves without hurting the very ones who give you life. Thank you.

Jefferson: Excellent. That was excellent! Did you enjoy sharing your message with us?

KwheelTravRiupaus: Yes. Very much so!

Jefferson: How many people do you have there with you?

KwheelTravRiupaus: Right now there are several thousands on the ship area.

Jefferson: No, but that are listening to our conversation?

KwheelTravRiupaus: It is just you and I.

Jefferson: I see. Wow. Okay. So, say hello to everyone. And... Do you understand then, why Treb does not really allow you to go any further with the information giving?

KwheelTravRiupaus: As soon as the ideas of technology comes along a signal is given that certain ideas that are beyond your understanding, should not be given to a race who is in this area of progression. And I understand that his beliefs are strong in this area. So I respect this and give you what you can have.

Jefferson: Right. Treb has the idea of non-interference. And I think for the most part he is right. Right?

KwheelTravRiupaus: Yes, in certain aspects correct.

Jefferson: In what aspect would you personally not agree, perhaps?

KwheelTravRiupaus: Giving you ideas of specific technologies that you can apply, without giving you the blueprint of how to do it fully. Only the idea and no directions to take. This can be very helpful for a race. But for him it is a different understanding.

Jefferson: Alright. So, hey, have a look! I thank you very much for your time and for your knowledge and for your wisdom. And it has been a delight to have had this opportunity to interact with you. Just before you go... how do you keep track of history in your planet?

KwheelTravRiupaus: There is a vocal system of communication that we have and there is an archive of all vocalizations of a specific point of interest for each member. And they record this into one large database.

Jefferson: So whenever everyone else wants to go there and listen, they just have to press a button and that is it.

KwheelTravRiupaus: To receive the information is not through spoken words. The spoken word is given to the machine and the machine makes it into a telepathic communication so telepathy is sent to you from voice to technology and from technology to telepathic waves and ideas.

Jefferson: So is Earth part of your story or history?

KwheelTravRiupaus: We have seen Earth, we have interacted with the area of your solar system many times but we have not directly connected to your people.

Jefferson: So I am the first human you spoke to.

KwheelTravRiupaus: Directly, yes.

Jefferson: So how is this interaction be inserted in your archives?

KwheelTravRiupaus: I will speak about our conversation and it will be recorded for others to experience if they wish to.

Jefferson: And in your level of understanding you can remember from beginning to end every word?

KwheelTravRiupaus: The general ideas, yes.

Jefferson: Oh alright. Okay, great. Once again, thank you very much. You have yourself a lovely life. And... uh... perhaps when I go back to in between lives, I may pay you a little visit. In less than eighty of our years I will be there. So...

KwheelTravRiupaus: Yes. This will be very exciting.

Jefferson: So, yes. So, thank you very much. I just so hope that when anybody reads this message a rainbow of love and light appears on your planet.

KwheelTravRiupaus: Thank you for this!

Jefferson: Thank you very much. Good bye for now.

*** [Silence]

Treb Bor yit-NE: Jefferson?

Jefferson: So Treb, Riupaus wanted to give me some ideas of technology. And you are not the only one who Treb doesn't really want that to come through. I would imagine that is because human beings must, in a sense, deserve it. Make their way onto it so that they can grow with and within that process. Is that why you do that?

Treb Bor yit-NE: Yes. This is one aspect of many. But if you are seeing the idea of the atomic bomb, or the hydrogen bomb, you are seeing technology that is more advanced than humanity and it is given to humanity in one way or another and using this in a way that is not correct has a very devastating impact to all entities who resides within this area. So if you are seeing technological aspects of a race who has technology before the time in which the technology should, or could be available to them, this is the result of this.

Jefferson: So basically the nuclear bomb was given either by spirits that were in between lives messing up, that were intellectually advanced but not morally or by some extraterrestrial race.

Treb Bor yit-NE: This aspect of this I wish not to... uh...

Jefferson: Get involved with!

Treb Bor yit-NE: Yes. I do not wish to speak of the intent of others.

Jefferson: Very good. You are very wise!

Treb Bor yit-NE: Uh... thank you.

Jefferson: This connection must be ended now so much love to you.

Treb Bor yit-NE: Yes. I will leave this connection now in love and in light and we will speak to each other very soon.

Jefferson: Very soon sir. Thank you.

Treb Bor yit-NE: Yes. Good bye.

Jefferson: Good bye.

TIHNAS-TOLAH HUMANS

Chapter 11
09/12/2012

Planet: Lahd-ieNacee
Lifespan: 600 years

Spokesperson: Iosoma
Age: 243 years old

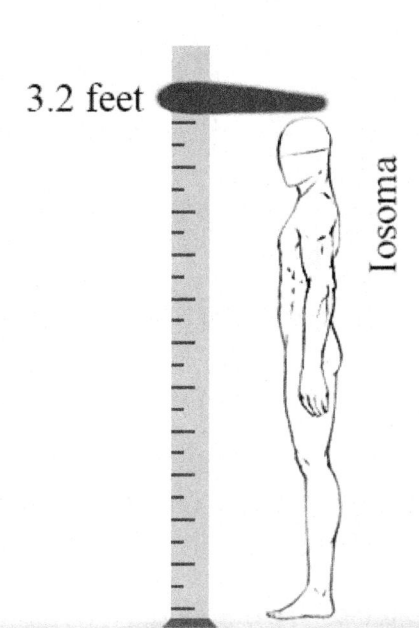

3.2 feet

Iosoma

Galactic Human: Hello Jefferson.

Jefferson: Indeed. How are you?

Galactic: Human: I am doing fantastic.

Jefferson: Who are you?

Galactic Human: My name is Iosoma.

Jefferson: Are you of a female orientation?

Iosoma: No.

Jefferson: So, it is left to me to assume you are of a male orientation. [Giggles]

Iosoma: [Giggles] That is very correct.

Jefferson: Wow. And... uh... well Treb just shared an idea with me that you were from a mother race?

Iosoma: Uh... I am not sure of the question.

Jefferson: Yeah. Me neither! Well, lets just move on. [Giggles]. So, what constellation are you from?

Iosoma: The way our sky is situated, it is the one that is called the dragon...

Jefferson: The dragon... hmm...

Iosoma: Draco... the dragon.

Jefferson: Alright. Thank you. And what is the name of your planet?

Iosoma: Our planet is Ladimasir

Jefferson: Would you say it again?

Iosoma: Lahd-ieNacee

Jefferson: What is the size of your planet? Is that as big as ours?

Iosoma: Do you know how big that yours is?

Jefferson: Yes.

Iosoma: Hmm... Treb says that is three fourths, or three fifths of yours.

Jefferson: In the sense that it is bigger?

Iosoma: Smaller!

Jefferson: Oh I see.

Iosoma: A three fractions of a five.

Jefferson: Wow. How long is a day for you?

Iosoma: For a whole revolution it is about twelve weeks.

Jefferson: Right. But I mean for one revolution around itself. One...

Iosoma: From the time that the sun appears until it comes again?

Jefferson: Yes.

Iosoma: It is twelve weeks of yours.

Jefferson: Wow. And how long is a year for you?

Iosoma: It is four and one half of your years.

Jefferson: Wow. So, what is the color of your skies?

Iosoma: When you are looking at the sky, there is a pink color.

Jefferson: How many people do you have in your planet?

Iosoma: We only have seven and one half millions.

Jefferson: Okay. If you are coming from outside, what is the color of your planet?

Iosoma: When you are looking down, it is very, very blue, and very, very orange.

Jefferson: Can you speak about your solar system set up?

Iosoma: There is one star and within the star... I am not sure how you classify these bodies... uh... a dwarfing! A brown dwarf. It is something that is more than a planet but less than a star. It has not yet achieved full fusion to make it a star, as a star? So there is one star and one of the dwarf browns. And in these dwarf browns and stars, they are going in the center and around the center, the first planet comes fairly close, the second planet comes a little further in an out-long angle and also a thirty one or thirty two degree tilt, while the others at a zero degrees, the first. And in the third planet, in which we are this is a circular orbit and on a four degree tilt.

Jefferson: Hmm. And what is the average temperature in your planet?

Iosoma: It is fifty one or fifty two degrees.

Jefferson: The source of light then for your planet are both of those ideas that you've just shared.

Iosoma: The dwarf does not give off a visible light in your

spectrum but it gives off light to our spectrum and also heat.

Jefferson: I see. What density are you?

Iosoma: We are in the fourth density.

Jefferson: How many moons do you have, if you do have any, around your planet?

Iosoma: There are twelve!

Jefferson: Why?

Iosoma: Very many small pieces of a larger piece. During collisions, it broke off into several smaller pieces. To our understanding, originally there was three of them and two of them collided breaking off into many smaller ones.

Jefferson: Wow. What makes a moon collide against another?

Iosoma: Apparently the gravitational pool from the planet and many on coming bodies would slightly alter its course and when the course is defined and there is a gravitational disruption then the course becomes undefined. And when it is undefined it can cross paths.

Jefferson: How are you guys in your society born?

Iosoma: We are born through sexual activities.

Jefferson: Right. But then, once mom and daddy have those lovely encounters, then the... is this like us perhaps? The baby is seeded and mom becomes pregnant.

Iosoma: Yes and once this occurs, then the child will be born, seven and eight half of your years later and once this is done then a child is born.

Jefferson: In the world of my future self (Pleenaki), once they have that sexual relationship they take off the little egg, fertilized egg and they leave the human physical body to grow in a specific particular tank designed for that idea. How does it work for you? Do you remain in your mom's womb all the time?

Iosoma: Uh... I am not sure what the womb is. Is this inside of the body?

Jefferson: Yes! Where the baby usually grows.

Iosoma: Yes there is an area in the lower stomach regions in which it grows for seven and one half years?

Jefferson: And how does it come out? Do you cut the mom's belly or just naturally?

Iosoma: There is no cutting. It is a natural mechanism that removes it from the body.

Jefferson: Right. Do you have doctors that study, specifically to help people throughout their pregnancy and the baby afterward?

Iosoma: No this is an instinctive setting from our race from long ago. And once we are impregnated as a person then we would give birth with no help. There is... it is just done whenever it is ready to come.

Jefferson: Wow. What do you look like?

Iosoma: We are about three feet tall, three and one half feet. And there is hair, it is brown and red. And we have various colors of skin patches on our hands. There are orange and red and pink. And this grow from the area from your hand, perhaps knuckle to the elbow and it is a light sprinkle of patterns and we each have this as well.

Jefferson: So, there is a pattern of colors that goes from your hand to your elbow.

Iosoma: Yes and each one is different in color and different in pattern.

Jefferson: And what about the rest of the body, what color is it?

Iosoma: It is a very, very light orange.

Jefferson: Hmm. And what is the color of your eyes?

Iosoma: There are magnitudes of colors. Everyone has a different color in a specific range. Even if they are similar, it is slightly different.

Jefferson: Tell me about colors as they sit on your body.

Iosoma: How do you mean?

Jefferson: What colors are you?

Iosoma: For me it is a light orange skin. I have a pink pattern from the arms and it is impossible to explain the amount of small marks on each arm with a precision. There are several thousand on each arm and there is orange hair and purple eyes and a very, very light orange color of skin. I am three feet and two inches.

Jefferson: Did you say orange hair?

Iosoma: Uh... maybe red as you would see it.

Jefferson: Red. Okay. Do you separate childhood to teenager and adulthood, in your planet?

Iosoma: Uh... there is a birth process. After this birth process, once integrated into the world, from the mother to the existing outside of the mother there is a full functionality of the body. And once this happens, there is two hundred year area that is of physical, emotional, mental and spiritual growth. And once this happens there is perhaps, what you see to be adulthood.

Jefferson: I see. How long can you stay in your human physical body?

Iosoma: Around six hundred years.

Jefferson: How old are you?

Iosoma: I am 243.

Jefferson: So you are about my age. A third way to the end.

Iosoma: Uh... yeah in between one third and one half.

Jefferson: Right. So, do you think... if you were to be seen on Earth, we would realize you are not from here? [Giggles]

Iosoma: I believe that this would be the case.

Jefferson: But I mean, of course because of your different coloration, not only for the skin but for the hair and for the eyes. But what I mean, really, is for the size of your nose, of your eyes, the way they are placed on your body, are those (as the host says) appendages different?

Iosoma: The nose structure is very similar to some of yours. I understand there is a wide variety of nose in your race too and sizes. But it is placed in the same area. It is similar by being elongated with two nostrils to breath. The eyes are slightly different. Yours tend to be in an elongated, not circular but ovular shape and ours tend to be a bit more rounded. And they are placed on the same area of the head but slightly higher on the head.

Jefferson: So do you think that the part that is close to the nose is lower or higher than the opposite side?

Iosoma: Uh... I am not understanding what you mean.

Jefferson: Do you think that... for instance you have your eyes and do you think that the part of your eyes that is closer to your nose, is lower... is it pointing down or upwards?

Iosoma: It doesn't point. They are quite circular. So there is no pointing.

Jefferson: Oh okay. Do you get old?

Iosoma: There is a time of death. And this is once the soul is old.

Jefferson: I see. So the body of your 200 year young adult is the same of your 600 year's.

Iosoma: Very similar! Much less contrast than your adulthood to your death time.

Jefferson: Understood. But there is some getting old there.

Iosoma: Yes. There is a difference. In the way that the body is becoming different sizes. Some get smaller and some larger. But not in the height. More in the area of the chest and legs.

Jefferson: What is the name of your race again?

Iosoma: The name of our planet is not the same as our race. I will give you the name of our planet.

Jefferson: Uh huh.

Iosoma: The planet's name is Lahd-ieNacee and of our race is called TihnasTolah.

Jefferson: TihnasTolah. Okay. Are men and women the same as far as looks?

Iosoma: Similar, just as in your race, they have very similar looks.

Jefferson: But are they similar also in the chest area?

Iosoma: Slightly! The woman's chest tend to be more broad in the upper areas.

Jefferson: Do they breast feed?

Iosoma: Oh! In this way? No. Men and women are the same.

They are not different.

Jefferson: Do you wear clothing?

Iosoma: We wear clothes that are white. It is one piece of clothes.

Jefferson: Do you have toilet trips? Does your body produce any waste?

Iosoma: No. Everything is used precisely as needed. There is no extra energies or extra manifestations of things within our energies.

Jefferson: Do you kiss one another?

Iosoma: No.

Jefferson: How do you show affection to the beloved one?

Iosoma: There is a song that is sang.

Jefferson: A song?!

Iosoma: Yes. Each individual will sing to another their song. A song to show their affection for the other.

Jefferson: But do you sing that to everyone you love or just to that specific person you want to marry with?

Iosoma: The concept of marriage is not the same either. But it is a song that is specific for each one we love showing them a different energy in expression of that love for your connection to them. Even though love is distributed quite equally, there is still differences in the relationships that we have with each individual. Each serves a different purpose and meaning.

Jefferson: So, is that the way you relate to music?

Iosoma: Oh yes! Very much so! It is a sharing of energy and love in connection. And it is expressed through a vocal changing of words and shifts in vibration.

Jefferson: How does the system of education work in your planet?

Iosoma: Education is something that has no structure. There is no specific way to do it. Each learns as they learn.

Jefferson: Do you have religion?

Iosoma: Uh... religion is not a concept we share here. There is no different ideas of a connection to a God. Only in the way that we experience it.

Jefferson: How do you see God?

Iosoma: For me, myself, personally... I see this God or idea of everything in the connections that we make and the forces that help us to motivate ourselves to become more excellent. And Also within the motivation to connect to others in specific ways. For instance, if I am connecting to someone outside of a planet that I never met, I would express many feelings of gratitude and love and I will take their energy and understand and we will join our energy. And this expression is that specific God, it is that specific connection to him or to her. This is the best way to describe it.

Jefferson: I see. Hmm. Do you like God?

Iosoma: There is no disliking in this because it is the emotional pattern that sets the motion. So there is no disliking or liking. It is in all things. Things we truly prefer and things we prefer less than that and things that we prefer average. And so every vibration from the lowest to the highest that we come in, this is the experience to God.

Jefferson: Do you think then that God is the supreme intelligence and the first cause of everything?

Iosoma: Perhaps not a supreme intelligence because we all have that connection, we all have the capability to know as he does. Because we are a part of that. And for the first cause of the physical aspect, yes. Most definitely! Because if it was not for him none of the physical reality that we are in would be valid.

Jefferson: Would you have a structure of government?

Iosoma: Government is also something we don't complicate or do not integrate into our society.

Jefferson: You don't need your society to be complicated do you?

Iosoma: No. Complications tend to complicate things.

Jefferson: [Laughter] Are your cities the same as ours?

Iosoma: No. There are many places to gather and there are many spread. We have a very large planet and a very small population. So we each have areas that we go to and leave and then we all connect at one point or another but there is no town, there is only dwellings.

Jefferson: Can you give us an idea of what your dwellings look like?

Iosoma: They are made from a rock and the large rocks that are used above ground. They tend to be a shelled out as a dome structure. And then we place whatever we wish inside of them to make them more personal to our own vibration. So it is a large, rounded structure. And if it is hollowed out and many things... for instance in mine, there are places to lay, there are places to sit, there are places to enjoy company. And there are also many... of the native plants, is how you would call them, that grow inside, from the ground. So it is very beautiful and the vibration is relaxing.

Jefferson: So can you get your house and take it to another planet if you wish?

Iosoma: It is possible. There are crafts that would be able to move it but it is a part of the planet. It is a part vibrationally. It keeps the same vibrational encoding.

Jefferson: Okay. Do you have pets?

Iosoma: No. There are animals. But... uh... not as pets. Only as projections of our own consciousness.

Jefferson: Which is the animal you like the most?

Iosoma: They are all very great! But one specifically, that tends to catch the heart of myself is a small flying animal. It is about the size of a human hand and it flies throughout the air.

Jefferson: So it has wings and feet and a beak.

Iosoma: No. This is more of a human animal, that you are speaking of correct?

Jefferson: Yeah.

Iosoma: This one has arms that are extended out. And they are similar to a bat. But they are not like a bat. They have a skin or membrane that connects from their arms to the bottom of their feet. But they tend to look more like a mammal of yours with no beak. They have a long face and they are able to fly.

Jefferson: Wow. And what color is that?

Iosoma: They are white, brown and green.

Jefferson: Do they have teeth?

Iosoma: They have little parts in their mouth in which they are able to chew up plants. They are not teeth but they are structures of bumps that have grindings much as sandpaper of yours. Only thicker.

Jefferson: Do they express their feelings?

Iosoma: They are always sharing their energy. Their way of expression if felt within the energy of them.

Jefferson: Do you have systems of transportation in your planet?

Iosoma: Yes. There are many sources of transportation. There are ones that go in the water and there are ones that leave the planet and there are also ones that go around the planet.

Jefferson: What is your job or passion and is it both one and the same in your particular race?

Iosoma: The passion is the same as the job, because there are no true jobs. There is only existence. But in this my favorite part is to come and study various second density life forms throughout the galaxies.

Jefferson: Wow. Uh... So, are you in the future?

Iosoma: I am not sure what you mean.

Jefferson: Can you ask Treb to help us out?

Iosoma: Yes. Yes. I will try to connect to him that way.

***[Silence]

Iosoma: Uh... he explains one, one, seven and eight.

Jefferson: Oh [Giggles] Thank you! How did you get this invitation?

Iosoma: While exploring other second densities lifeforms upon a planet that the measurement of systems... Uh.... Parsecs! That was four and a half of the Parsecs, from my planet, I was looking at the second density life and I felt a presence and I connected to it and it was the one that you called Treb.

Jefferson: Why do you think you felt it, and not other people?

Iosoma: At that point I was on the planet by myself with the second density life form, exploring them and looking at them. And when I felt the presence I connected to it instantly, so there was no others in the direct vicinity to feel this.

Jefferson: Oh, so you were by yourself in that place, not in the entire planet.

Iosoma: Within the fourth density or of fifth, or sixth until Treb had come by in his consciousness I was alone. Only the second densities and first densities were there with me.

Jefferson: Understood. But when you say alone, what do you mean? Did they left on vacation to another solar system?

Iosoma: This planet is not inhabited yet by any life other than the first and the second.

Jefferson: So you are not in your planet right now.

Iosoma: I am now, yes.

Jefferson: So this planet is inhabited by your people.

Iosoma: Yes. But the connection was received one and one half of your days ago.

Jefferson: Right. Oh understood! So you were in a different planet them.

Iosoma: Yes.

Jefferson: I see, thank you.

Iosoma: You are welcome.

Jefferson: I feel that you are exceptionally excited to talk to us. Why is that?

Iosoma: I find great interest. Although you are not a second density entity, you are a very, very in tune with your second density life as far as the variety in your planet and how much energy of a second density nature is connected to your energy directly.

Jefferson: Wow. So, would you like then, to share with us the message that you have from you and your planet today?

Iosoma: Yes. I would love to share my message.

Jefferson: Okay. So, just before you do, how many people do you have there?

Iosoma: With me specifically now? There are twelve.

Jefferson: Okay. Alright. So... yeah. Let us hear your message please.

Iosoma: I wish to greet Earth, properly, in whatever way it is proper for humans. I wish to greet you in that way. And I also wish to express ideas of love and connection with you and while you are exchanging the energy with me I wish to talk about something that I love with you. You have a great many entities that are on your planet that some humans tend to see as less than them. Some humans tend to see below them. That they are only animals, that they are only second density beings. I wish you to have an understanding made with you about these entities.

    Although these entities are several times smaller in

consciousness than a third density being, they are still a projection of your consciousness, just as you are projection of your fourth density consciousness and as they are projections of the fifth, and continuously down, the connections go both ways. So although they are smaller they are still equal to you. They are still a part of you. To see them in a way that you would wish for other races to see you, if you believe them to be superior in knowledge, if you are able to sympathize with them on this level, or even empathize with them on this level, perhaps the idea of those who do not treat them well and do not show them love and see them to be equals, perhaps this will be balanced.

I wish not to show you judgment or discern for your race, only an understanding, only to share the knowledge that we have. And I understand that some of you will use it to change your view and some of you will not. But these entities are a part of you. Just as your children are a part of you and you would not with any harm on the children. So if you are able to see them in this light, perhaps it will help you more greatly to understand that all consciousness feels and all consciousnesses connects. You just have to find your right setting within your heart to connect to them. And I wish to leave you all in great joy of abundant love and connection to you and to your second density and first density beings on your planet. Thank you.

Jefferson: Wow. Thank you very much. How did you enjoy sharing your message?

Iosoma: It was very exciting.

Jefferson: It was excellent! Thank you very much for that. Did you know that in our planet there are animals that eat us, if we let it.

Iosoma: I've heard about this in some places, yes.

Jefferson: Yeah! And there are animals that bite us if we don't kick them.

Iosoma: Yes. [Laughter]

Jefferson: So... it is perhaps the conditioning and it is our own fault, but still!

Iosoma: It is a co-creation. One needs to be bitten and the other needs to bite.

Jefferson: [Laughter] Alright. So, amongst those twelve people there, is there anyone in particular that has had more contact with Earth in a general way?

Iosoma: Not directly no.

Jefferson: But has anyone who has studied it more or you are the one who is more connected to us in general?

Iosoma: We all have a general understanding of Earth. We also have a general love for your planet. But not a deep understanding in a way of some that study your race. This is not like that.

Jefferson: Do you have any particular question you want to ask before we end this transmission?

Iosoma: One moment, I will collect the thoughts and I will feel them all.

Jefferson: Alright.

***[Silence]

Iosoma: The idea in question that is given is, where do you believe that your race will be in thirty years if the energy stays the exact same and does not progress.

Jefferson: Well, the idea that the energy will stay the same is, for a being at the level of consciousness where I am, is somewhat impossible. But let's say it changes on to the same thing over and over. Then we will probably learn the hard way how to become a civilized society. But I do believe that in the end, for good or for worse, we are going to get through the tough times and then in thirty years we are going for sure, to be part of the Association of Worlds or, if you will, the Interstellar Alliance. In that I extend the invitation for your race, if you feel like, and in case we are already part of the fourth density, for you guys to come about and pay us a visit!

Iosoma: That is very, very great invitation. And the general consensus of the thirteen of us is that you are very wise and that you understand the energy never stays the same.

Jefferson: [Laughter]. Thanks.

Iosoma: And this is very great! And we wish to express to you that in the end it all works out as it should and you have a great existence!

Jefferson: Wow. Thank you very much. You yourself as well. Before you go, tell me, how are you connecting to us? I know it is through Treb but do you have your eyes closed? Do you need the craft to help you boost your energy?...

Iosoma: There is a mechanism which has a crystal of the imprints of each hand and we stand and place our hands there to help produce the energy in a more stable way, to project it.

Jefferson: Wow. That is interesting! Alright, So, you take care and let's create a wish that every time someone reads whatever we have spoken about in the information we've shared, a rainbow of love and light appears in your planet as means of myself and my planet to express our gratitude for your time and your wisdom.

Iosoma: Uh... What is a rainbow?

Jefferson: A rainbow is...

Iosoma: Oh! Yes. ***[Treb just helped Iosoma]. Oh! This is a very great thought! And it is greatly appreciated!!

Jefferson: Right. [Laughter]. So, yes. Thank you very much you have a lovely existence. And perhaps, because you live 600 years or about, in less than 90 years I will be in between lives, in the spiritual world, preparing for my next embodiment, and I will, if I am allowed, I will pay you a visit in your planet, in spirit.

Iosoma: This would be a very great visit. And if your consciousness does not achieve the level where you are able to project, well then perhaps we will come to see you!

Jefferson: Fantastic, do it!

Iosoma: Yes this will be very great!

Jefferson: Thank you very much.

Iosoma: Thank you for your blessing of connection and love.

Jefferson: Likewise. You are adorable! Good bye.

Iosoma: Thank you, good bye.

$ΩWKWANTY HUMAN$

Chapter 12
10/01/2012

Planet: Kwiltar
Lifespan: 15000 years

Spokesperson: Dwantelgo
Age: 5789 years old

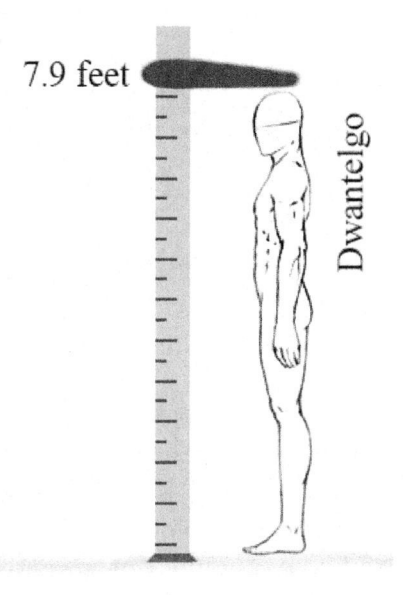

7.9 feet — Dwantelgo

Galactic Human: Greetings to you Jefferson.

Jefferson: Greeting to you too! Hello from Earth. Who are you?

Galactic Human: My name is Dwontelgo.

Jefferson: Dontelgo?

Galactic Human: Dwan-telgo.

Jefferson: Ah, Dwantelgo.

Dwantelgo: Yes.

Jefferson: What constellation are you?

Dwantelgo: Constellation?... uh... from your planet, in the southern skies?... It is a serpent's name... Hydra.

Jefferson: Hydra...

Dwantelgo: It is the largest star in the Hydrus system.

***[Hydra is the largest of the 88 modern constellations, measuring 1303 square degrees. Also one of the longest at over 100 degrees, its southern end abuts Libra and Centaurus and its northern end borders Cancer. It has a long history, having been included among the 48 constellations listed by the 2nd century astronomer Ptolemy. It is commonly represented as a water snake. It should not be confused with the similarly named constellation of Hydrus. Source: Wikipedia.]

Jefferson: What is the name of your planet?

Dwantelgo: The name of our planet... it is called Kwiltar.

Jefferson: Kwilta?

Dwantelgo: Kwiltar, with the R.

Jefferson: Kwiltar.

Dwantelgo: Yes.

Jefferson: And what is the name of the race?

Extraterrestrial Life

Dwantelgo: The Sowkwanty.

Jefferson: Okay. Hey, what is the size of your planet? Is that as big as ours?

Dwantelgo: It is larger than yours. Approximately three times.

Jefferson: Wow. And how long is a day for you there?

Dwantelgo: It is approximately twice the length of your day.

Jefferson: I see. What is the color of your skies?

Dwantelgo: It is a very dark blue.

Jefferson: Wow. How many people do you have in your planet?

Dwantelgo: Approximately 137 million.

Jefferson: Uh huh. And if you are coming from the outside what is the color of the planet?

Dwantelgo: It is... uhh... if you are coming down and if you are close, sitting above it is a mixture of colors of dark, green, dark blue and light blue.

Jefferson: What is the set up for your solar system?

Dwantelgo: We have a singular star as you do. Approximately twice the size of your star. It is white in color. There are eleven planets that surround this. We are the fifth planet from the beginning to the end if you are going from the closest to the stars to the furthest. We are the fifth. On all of these planets, there are abundance of life. There are two planets that inhabit third density races. There are four that inhabit second density. There is one that inhabits something larger than ourselves. And also one planet that holds two races of the fifth densities.

Jefferson: What is that thing that is larger than yourselves. A dinosaur?

Dwantelgo: Uh... larger in consciousness, not in physical sense.

Jefferson: Oh, I see. Do you mean more evolved?

Dwantelgo: Perhaps if you contrast large consciousness to evolution, then yes.

Jefferson: How many moons do you have?

Dwantelgo: Four moons.

Jefferson: I see. Why?

Dwantelgo: Uh... the beginning of our planet and evolution, dictated that four must come with our planet.

Jefferson: I understand. What is then the functions of the moons?

Dwantelgo: Uh... there is no specific function for these, but if you see, as on your planet, your one moon holds the access to be in a very specific pattern so that life may evolve. This is not necessary on our planet.

Jefferson: Oh I see. Uh... There is a purpose though, right?

Dwantelgo: Yes. For all things there are purposes.

Jefferson: Do you know by any chance the purpose of having four moons instead of one?

Dwantelgo: Four our idea of why they are there, we understand the mechanics very well.

Jefferson: I see. And uh... what is the average temperature in your planet?

Dwantelgo: 40 degrees of your Fahrenheit range.

Jefferson: Wow. It is pretty cold! So, what density are you?

Dwantelgo: We are in what you would know to be the fifth density.

Jefferson: Right. What is the main difference between fifth and fourth?

Dwantelgo: There are quite a few differences. But the main differences are on harmonic levels, higher frequency of material that is made. But also evolution that is beyond only the want and need to experience love in a full cycle. As we have done this already with our race, we moved to another cycle. We begin a cycle of learning and knowledge. We begin incorporating all of the love that we have used and the material, technology that we received in the previous density and we build upon this, expanded into different realms and different areas of our galaxy, quite largely. Within the galaxy we have traveled throughout most of it.

Jefferson: So the idea then is that you are, for those on the fourth density less physical but for those in your density you are as physical.

Dwantelgo: Correct. We are as physical as you are within yours and the fourth are within theirs. But the idea of ones below our densities, then this would be seen to be very non-physical or semi-physical.

Jefferson: Right. And for you in the fifth density, when you look at us we are then just as physical but of a different vibrating frequency.

Dwantelgo: Yes. Your matter is much more compacted.

Jefferson: Denser?!

Dwantelgo: Correct.

Jefferson: Uh huh. I see. And then... but do you have the same obstacles to overcome matter in your density? Say for instance you have a wall, because the wall is made of your materials then it is as thick or impenetrable as it would be for us the walls that are built up in our frequency.

Dwantelgo: If we were not able to transport the physical self from one area to the other without having to walk through this wall, then yes, it would be physical and unstoppable. But because our consciousness is more complex, we are able to want to be on the other side of the wall and then appear there.

Jefferson: Right so that is the same equation I have spoken about before, I am not sure if you are aware, I don't think so. That... uh... location is a variable of your energy signature. So what you do you just change the variable location of the equation of your being and then you stop being in this place where you are and you start being somewhere else.

Dwantelgo: Uh... this is actually a very good representation of the ability to move our consciousness.

Jefferson: Did you expect that coming from a third density being? [Giggles]

Dwantelgo: Uh... if you were not able to make equations within your mind that fit higher ways of thinking, then you would not be speaking to a member of a fifth density race. So that is very much respected.

Jefferson: Wow. I take that as a compliment! [Giggles] Thank you.

Dwantelgo: You are very welcome.

Jefferson: So, how are you guys born?

Dwantelgo: We are manifested into a physical structure that is made by a physical material compressed into a small area. As this physical material of living tissue is compressed it has time to incubate itself into a physical structure of a body and then our consciousness is directly transported into this being.

Jefferson: So you are created outside of a human physical body.

Dwantelgo: Yes. This is correct. There is no internal sexual connections as you have.

Jefferson: So do you have what we call scientists to manipulate genetics of mom and daddy?

Dwantelgo: Our whole race is capable of this feats.

Jefferson: So basically if you want to have a baby, yourself, you just go to the "kitchen" and you do one.

Dwantelgo: Not in the same area that we manifest our food.

Jefferson: I know. [Giggles] But I mean, in a place that you, yourself... you create one.

Dwantelgo: Oh yes. Correct!

Jefferson: So, how do you do it? Do you get the energy from female and from male and put them together and put in a particular place for it to grow and you wait until it is fully grown and then you release it?

Dwantelgo: Yes, it is a... in a simple answer... yes.

Jefferson: Right. But it is a little more complex than that, of course.

Dwantelgo: Yes. There are several rituals that we have for a specific matching of the male and the female. To both manifest this physical body.

Jefferson: Can you speak of one? Do you for instance dance around each other...

Dwantelgo: No. There are vibrations always coming from an area in our planet that is mountainous so that it has consistent flow of air that comes from the bottom of the ground out to small openings and they are making different harmonic tones, so there is always great sound. Much as a low trumpet, or a...

perhaps a trombone but not as sounding as brass, coming more from a natural flow. So it is a large deep whistling. And everyone of these tones are different as the cycles of the planet are different. And as the pressure of the air is different the tones become different. Once a tone matches a specific vibrational cord within the female, then she will find a male that is close to her at this timing and then they will connect with a specific child taking matter of both parents, connecting it to a child.

Jefferson: And then once that connection is made, is what we call on Earth conception.

Dwantelgo: Correct.

Jefferson: But then, how long does it take for it to grow enough in order for it to be able to stand on its own and walk amongst you?

Dwantelgo: To be able to have all physical functions?

Jefferson: Yes.

Dwantelgo: Approximately 128 years.

Jefferson: Wow. Is there then a time that separates childhood from becoming a teenager and then an adult and so on?

Dwantelgo: Uh... there is... if you break into three stages as your race would: childhood, teenager and adult... uh... then within the physical trait from being a child is 128 approximately to be able to walk and learn all of the things that the physical body needs to be able to take care of itself. From this time to 1000 years approximately... uh... this is a growing up time. And from 1000 to 3000, this is the time of learning. After 3000 until you are done with the cycle, done with your incarnation cycle, somewhere in the area of 15000 of your years, this is all adulthood.

Jefferson: How long can you stay in your physical body?

Dwantelgo: Uh... approximately 15000 of your years.

Jefferson: I see and how old are you?

Dwantelgo: 5789 perhaps.

Jefferson: So you are about my age, I mean you are a third on your way to bend space.

Dwantelgo: Correct.

Jefferson: I see. And what do you look like?

Dwantelgo: We are... in your heights it would be 7.9 inches, approximately.

Jefferson: Okay. Uh huh. Do you look human like us?

Dwantelgo: Oh, very much so.

Jefferson: So if you were to come down here and walk amongst us... I know we would be unable to see you because you exist in a different frequency of reality but, taking aside this particular, if we were to be able to see you waking amongst us as a third density being, would we realize you are from a different planet by your looking?

Dwantelgo: If you are to take my height in consideration, this would alone place me outside of the normality but if height were just as yours, there would be no way to distinguish me.

Jefferson: Wow. What is your skin color?

Dwantelgo: Uh... it is very close to a race that has... the one that resides in Spain, Spaniards.

Jefferson: Right. Well... I don't think that would help a lot. But... uh... because Brazilians are somewhat very different as well and yet similar to all races. But lets talk in these terms: from 0 being black and 100 being white, where do you locate your skin color in that scale?

Dwantelgo: Close to 60 or 65.

Jefferson: Great. That is great, that is a clear answer. So, what is the color of your eyes?

Dwantelgo: They are dark blue.

Jefferson: Dark blue. Is that the same for everybody?

Dwantelgo: No. There are varieties of blue.

Jefferson: I see. But no yellow, no green...

Dwantelgo: No they are from one side of the spectrum of blue to the next or to the very far end of the next.

Jefferson: I see. And do you get old?

Dwantelgo: No. The physical body does not change much from

the time that it is fully developed at 1000.

Jefferson: Are men and women the same? Do they look the same?

Dwantelgo: There are similarities and there are also differences. The differences are being... the area that is known to be the breast, that your race would consider breast, the milk feeding areas.

Jefferson: Right.

Dwantelgo: These have stayed with us through our race. At this area of our existence we are put back into our original race's looks as we get ready to graduate into the sixth density, our looks have changed back to the original looks of our third density and second density animals.

Jefferson: Like... like... animals as we are animals, right?

Dwantelgo: No, as a second density is considered to be an animal. I am using terms that I will hope that you understand, yes.

Jefferson: Okay. So what do you mean by our looks changed back to second density looks?

Dwantelgo: As races go towards a full understanding of not only love, but also learning much wisdom, then they come to a place that you would know to be a sixth density being. Once this occurs they are using all of the love that they have gotten from the fourth density and all of the wisdom within the fifth and combine this to spread out larger areas of consciousness and also to be able to share this with other races and other beings. We are coming close to this area, the sixth density. And when you are in the sixth density, many races tend to revert back to the animal version of themselves, in the physical way of looking. Because this is their original essence of being. In the first density you do not have a physical characteristic because you are small portions of consciousness but once the consciousness is raised to elevation of self awareness, this is where the true beginning of an evolution of consciousness starts. Therefore we revert back to this look.

Jefferson: Right, so when you get to the sixth density, what do you look like? A cat?

Dwantelgo: For us it is very much like your race looks now.

Jefferson: Oh, I see.

Dwantelgo: A very human look. We have always looked human in nature. But in the fourth density there was no need for breast because there was nobody being fed. And as our race continues to evolve this look comes back into the original of our second density animal which was much like a human but not with such a large portion of consciousness. For your race, the animal that you came from tends to look more as a monkey.

Jefferson: Right.

Dwantelgo: But for our race our animal looks more like a human did.

Jefferson: Okay. [Laughter]

Dwantelgo: Less intelligent, less consciousness and less aware.

Jefferson: Alright. Thanks. So, do you wear clothing?

Dwantelgo: Yes, we wear. There are many different varieties of clothing. Depending on the individual but most of us has regressed to our beginning of third density clothing appearance. Which is much as robes or over dressings that are complete on the body for the size.

Jefferson: What does your hair looks like?

Dwantelgo: Just like yours, in texture, in size of the average human. It is one that is long to the area of the... your area of the buttocks and it is black in color.

Jefferson: So yours is black as well. And the ears are the same.

Dwantelgo: Correct.

Jefferson: Okay and did you have pets?

Dwantelgo: There are no pets but we do have projections of second density animals here.

Jefferson: Uh huh. Which is the one animal you like the most?

Dwantelgo: There is one that is similar to your dear but it is much larger and it has a thick fur. Very thick fur.

Jefferson: Do you eat or drink?

Dwantelgo: We manifest a very small amount of energetic... which would appear to you as if they are... uh... almost as your berries are? They are round, but they do not share the characteristics of a berry. They do not have seeds they do not have insides... they are all full. And it is a small portion of consciousness that is made into the food. This is manifested by our consciousness. Understanding who you have connected to. To connect to me, he (Treb) wants to give you a similarity from his previous conversations with you, and this is the manifested liquid that they use on their planet *(see more on our book: Benevolent Hybrid Reptilian Humans). It is the same as this, the only difference is the visual representation.

Jefferson: I see. Does your body produce waste?

Dwantelgo: No this is not done.

Jefferson: Do you kiss one another?

Dwantelgo: There is no kissing.

Jefferson: Any touching at all?

Dwantelgo: Yes, there are ways to communicate through a physical touch.

Jefferson: How does education happen in your planet?

Dwantelgo: All information is directly absorbed through this period of growing up. From the time the body is physical and able to walk to the 1000 years, all information is directly... uh... how would you express that idea? To... to be able to... place information directly into one's mind, with no means of communication. It is directly placed there.

Jefferson: It is like a download of information.

Dwantelgo: Yes, this is the best word that fits the idea.

Jefferson: Do you have religion?

Dwantelgo: No, religion is not something that our race would resonate with.

Jefferson: How do you see God?

Dwantelgo: We see God as a greater portion of ourselves. There are several levels of consciousness that are higher than us. But it is us in a larger version. We are the smaller portions of this God.

Jefferson: So let's say that God is then... the supreme intelligence and first cause of everything in that it is the destination of every living, breathing and progressing soul.

Dwantelgo: Yes. This is a great way to explain this.

Jefferson: Lovely! What is the meaning of life for you?

Dwantelgo: Life is a chance that we are given to go from a non-physical entity to a physical to be able to experience one portion of many that we need to progress our soul to a full array.

Jefferson: And then going back into the non-physical and expanding your consciousness towards perfection.

Dwantelgo: Correct.

Jefferson: Well, I could be a fifth density being, right? [Laughter]

Dwantelgo: Yes you have very great knowledge.

Jefferson: Nah, I am just kidding!

Dwantelgo: It is not that your race does not carry this knowledge, but it has removed the ability to connect with that will.

Jefferson: Uh huh. What... okay. So, I understand that you relate to sound, since you spoke about the idea of your birthing process.

Dwantelgo: Yes.

Jefferson: But other than that way, is there any other way that you relate to music, to sound?

Dwantelgo: Oh yes. There are many musical instruments played and we enjoy music very much in our race.

Jefferson: Which instrument do you play?

Dwantelgo: I am able to play every instrument that we have, as do all of us.

Jefferson: Oh yes, you said.

Dwantelgo: But the one of preference is one that would sound very much as your wooden pipes. The old... uh... pen flute?, is what they would call this on your planet.

Jefferson: Flute?

Dwantelgo: Yes. A pen flute. Different sections of wood in different areas. And you are blowing each one to make a sound?

This is very much the same but it is with one metallic pipe.

Jefferson: Okay, thanks. Do you have a system of government?

Dwantelgo: No, there is no government.

Jefferson: Why?

Dwantelgo: There is no need for a government. All of us do as we need to progress further in this ourselves as a race but also smaller portion of a larger consciousness within our galaxy, expanding within the universe.

Jefferson: Do you have cities?

Dwantelgo: There are dwellings. There are places that there are more dwellings than others but we do not see it in this way. We do not have local groups where everyone lives at one area. We live anywhere we wish to. We live in our dwellings.

Jefferson: Who makes these houses?

Dwantelgo: They are manifested through pure consciousness. As does all physical material. The knowledge of house manifesting, the specific energy and concepts that we need to manifest a specific dwelling? This is given to you very early. So, once you are ready to dwell anywhere you wish, you are able to manifest one in an instant fashion.

Jefferson: Can you give us an idea of what a "city" or one of your houses look like?

Dwantelgo: There are dwellings that have several walls. Each individual wall is the exact same size, except for the one end.

The one end is twice as long as the other portions. They are approximately 12 feet in length, 100 feet in width and approximately 75 feet of depth to it.

Jefferson: Do you paint it?

Dwantelgo: There are multiple colors. Depending on each consciousness, on the outside and inside are given different colors as representations of the ones who are within the dwelling.

Jefferson: Right. Do you have systems of transportation?

Dwantelgo: There is only one transportation that we use. And this is a craft, if you will.

Jefferson: Right. So it is a space craft. What does it look like?

Dwantelgo: It is a perfect circular sphere.

Jefferson: Oh, like a ball.

Dwantelgo: Correct.

Jefferson: I see. What is your job or passion in your race? And is it both one and the same?

Dwantelgo: If you look at what I do and you consider this to be a job then yes. I only do as I wish to do, as my passion does. And this is to explore the galaxy, to meet other entities in physical nature and to meet other entities in a communication such as this in a non-physical way. Both of them excite me greatly!

Jefferson: Right, if you were to come to my planet and visit me you would need to wear your spiritual body with the frequency that makes the energy of the fourth and then with the frequency that makes the energy of the third. So you would basically have to put two "cloakings" over you in order to be seeing here and interact with us, right?

Dwantelgo: Correct! It would be a downsizing of the consciousness and a manifestation of a smaller portion, energetically, physically...

Jefferson: Right. Okay. So basically your consciousness is so evolved that a human physical body (such as ours from the third density) can no longer hold it.

Dwantelgo: Yes. But this is the way all entities above your density are.

Jefferson: Alright.

Dwantelgo: Yes. This is a specific energy. And as you understand, with your knowledge of consciousness it is implied that you would understand, even within a human form, there are many levels of consciousness, other ones in which are most great, tend to die at a young age because their consciousness is no longer able to fit in physical form.

Jefferson: Alright. Are you in the future?

Dwantelgo: No, there is a presence of time.

Jefferson: What do you mean?

Dwantelgo: I am not any time further than you are. I am now as we speak.

Jefferson: Oh. Okay. How did you get this invitation?

Dwantelgo: There was an understanding from an entity that is known to be Treb, for your race you call it Treb. He is one that I have known a long time ago.

Jefferson: Oh I see. So is like buddies with you.

Dwantelgo: We have a very great line of communications... approximately 120 of your years ago. There was a great communication that I have made.

Jefferson: Look, in 90 years from today, how old will you be?

Dwantelgo: In 90 years my age will be 5879.

Jefferson: So when you get at that age, I will be already in between lives. You know. I will be... my physical body will be gone and I will become a spirit.

Dwantelgo: Correct.

Jefferson: Do you think I will be able to go and visit you in spirit in your planet.

Dwantelgo: If you call for me I will be able to come to see you and if you come to see my race you would be able visit that portion of our planet. Because our planet has also exists in many different levels. Our consciousness... you would be able to see a lower fourth density version of our planet.

Jefferson: Right.

Dwantelgo: And if you were to come there, and you were to use a mindset to connect to the Sowkwanty or even specifically to myself, then you will understand the connection that can be made. It is not one as if there would be a physical meeting or even one that you would think a non-physical but there will be an energy exchange.

Jefferson: Right. Because on my level of consciousness I can only interact with those that I resonate with.

Dwantelgo: This is correct. And as far as it is with resonance, you may resonate with many entities who are higher level of consciousness and you will interact with them, but not in a way that most would think. Because your consciousness, perhaps, is higher than many humans, uh... let us use an example. If you are a level 10 of 10 and you are able to communicate with ones within the fourth density that are on the lower levels of this, but because your physical body has died, now you are in the level 15. Because your level of consciousness is staying at a level where you are able to learn and grow as a non-physical entity. If you remain within the third density vibrational setting, in between lives, there will be no room to grow.

Jefferson: I see. So basically, it is not only that I am unable to visit places and speak to people that are on the fifth density, it is just... it is really not of my interest since they function in a way that is foreigner to me to the point of I being... really, being unable understand what is going on and benefiting from it.

Dwantelgo: Yes. There is much to be learned but these basic learnings can be taught to you by ones who are much closer to your vibrational learning in a way that will benefit you.

Jefferson: So basically, if I go to the spiritual world and I call for you, you would be able to come and visit me in spirit.

Dwantelgo: I would be able to communicate with you. As far as visiting it will depend on what level your consciousness is at and if you are able to see me.

Jefferson: Oh, I see. Wow. It is pretty complex but it seems to... it seems there is an order that is created with perfection so that we could all grow, learn with one another and teach one another.

Dwantelgo: Yes. This is correct.

Jefferson: Wow. So, how are you connecting right now, with me? I know it is through Treb, but do you have the help of any technology in your planet or how does it work for you there?

Dwantelgo: Oh no. I am only using a small portion of my consciousness to make this connection. As the one you know to be Treb, he is of a higher consciousness level and the ones that you might have spoke with in the previous times, the ones within the fourth density... they are in much greater need of a boost of consciousness to connect to Treb in a way that is useful to you and to your connection. But as for me I am at the higher or same level of consciousness as the one you call Treb. So there is not much consciousness that needs to have attention put to it to be able to make this connection.

Jefferson: For an evolved being such as yourself, what was the interest to talk to me and my race?

Dwantelgo: The interest is always the same. That you are one next piece of a larger puzzle to be put together. What I do is I learn. And everything that I learn has its place. Everything that I do there is lessons to be had, or a piece of information to be understood. This is one more, one next piece of the puzzle of learning all that I am able to learn.

Jefferson: Wow. And you are definitely then following your heart and allowing synchronicity to take you to the next step of your personal evolution where you can also, not only learn but teach.

Dwantelgo: Correct. The benefit of all can be had by learning and teaching.

Jefferson: Fantastic! I will step aside for a moment and invite you then to go ahead and share with us your most expected message for us.

Dwantelgo: Yes. My message for humans is very short and very much to the idea that I wish to express my love towards your race. But not only my love. Many race's love. You see many races that are coming to your planet now and this sometimes causes fear amongst certain humans. This is not a time to fear. It is a time to embrace the love that is given to you. When you receive love, than you are able to give love and once you are able to do this, then you are doing what you are meant to be: a conduit of love for information and also for conscious growth. And I wish to be a great part of this by sending my love and hopping that you will accept it.

Jefferson: We do! We will. And I really hope we understand not only the message that you shared but all of the races who have spoken to me who have taken from their precious time and understanding to share with us so that we can also grow as one as an equality within this idea of family. Adding not only to your puzzle but to ours so that we can also see the big picture, loving one another and participating in whatever way we may be concerned in our ability to build whatever we can within and as creation.

Dwantelgo: Yes. This is a very well understood idea and very well placed.

Jefferson: So thank you very much for your timelessness. I enjoyed this interaction immensely.

Dwantelgo: As have I.

Jefferson: So I will try and see if I can get and talk to you once I go back to the spiritual world in less than 90 years. But until then lets see what happens and you have an adorable life yourself. And once again, thank you so much for talking to us.

Dwantelgo: Thank you as well and may love be with you!

Jefferson: Thanks.

Dwantelgo: Good bye.

Jefferson: Good bye.

***[Silence]

Treb Bor yit-NE: Uh... yes Jefferson.

Jefferson: Hey Treb.

Treb Bor yit-NE: I hope that this was a great connection for you, for you to be able to use to help other with.

Jefferson: It was and I thank you very much for supporting and assisting us in all of these connections. It has certainly given us the opportunity to see how great, in the sense of awesome and also great in the sense of huge, immense, the universe is and how many portions of ourselves there are that we have no idea of.

Treb Bor yit-NE: Yes. I am very grateful to be a part of your connections to this for your own growth and for growth of all who wish for you to share with. And for all of those who wish to look at this.

Jefferson: So I thank you once again and I will leave you as you always leave us! In love and light and in appreciation for the knowledge we have acquired with this book and all the riches we now have thanks to these connections.

Treb Bor yit-NE: Yes and your gratitude is well accepted and also the gratitude for yourself for being able to be one who has an open mind and one who has an open heart and is able to receive such information to use to benefit all others. And I will leave you also in love and in light. We will speak to you very soon.

Jefferson: Thank you very much.

Treb Bor yit-NE: You are welcome. Good bye.

Jefferson: Good bye.

ABOUT THE AUTHORS
ROB GAUTHIER
http://www.trebchanneling.com

I was born in 1980. In 2007 I went to a spiritualism church. I went there because I decided to get my life back on track. I was looking into the dark for too long. Now I went there because this was the only place in the area that I could express my beliefs openly and meditate and be taught by many, many great psychics. As a child I was blessed with psychic abilities but as I digressed so did they. As I started learning from the great psychics in my area I learned many things. Including many experiences that I had as a child which were not figments of "just my imagination". And when I had thought I met my grandmother for the first time when I was nine, after she had been dead for over twenty years, I was right. This all started making sense to me. Something made me continue. So I continued to learn more meditations and after a couple years of working with my abilities every day, and really being dedicated about them, I met Treb Bor yit-NE.

I remember the first night I met him. I met him one night as I had a very usual night of feeling so disconnected from everything. I had been working on myself so hard and I looked at the night sky and knew that there is so much out there. I felt like I was in a prison (a great and beautiful one) on Earth. I just felt so much more should be felt. So I went into a deep meditation. That night I went further into my consciousness than I have ever gone before. I knew I had gone beyond the level of just going out of the body. I met him! And as he stood before me, the empty feeling I had before meditating, and the otherwise worried feeling I should had while seeing this huge odd looking alien, vanished. All I felt was love and happiness. I asked him who he was and he stared, talking to me.

He explained that reality wasn't how I saw it and that there is so much more to the universe. He also told me that I can take my newly found meditation ability and use it to permanently remove that loneliness. I did feel so alone. He also told me there was so much more evolution in not just the physical ideas, meaning that of the soul. I asked him about many things like the after life and his people.

After he answered me, and we met for the third time, I asked him, "what can I do to know if you are real, or a part of my mind?", he replied, "talk to this individual (a friend of mine)." I didn't know why. My friend had no knowledge of anything, I mean I would have known if he did, I would have heard. So I did, and he led me to a video, that led me to a book called "Seth Speaks, the Eternal Validity of the Soul" by Jane Roberts. I cried that day. The reason? ...even though it's greatly seen as very different views, all the information was so much alike; they were similar in very many ways. And then I figured I had my answer (also through many other synchronicities I would need a book to write them all). Since then, I have built a relationship of trust and respect with this brother of space. Now I feel it is my duty to share the information Treb Bor Yit-NE is willing to impart to our humanity. Information that saved me, sparing a lot of unnecessary psychological and physical suffering and delusions which I would definitely have gone through otherwise. I wish you all the same, a life fully lived with love and light (as Treb says), and that is how I wish to serve in my humble way too as I allow myself to be the host, the intermediary between him and us. As I have shared information now for over two years, I hope that it will affect positively and better your lives, as it has mine.

JEFFER$ON VI$CARDI
www.jeffersonviscardi.com

I was born in 1980. Once I learned about the french philosopher Dr. Kardec, Allan and the knowledge shared by the highly evolved spirits through several mediums (codified by him in five books to create the Spiritist Doctrine), I became fond of the wisdom of the immortality of the soul and its progressive evolution through many embodiments on many planets on its quest for perfection.

As a result of this life changing event I have been but focused and "entertained" by such a vast universe of possibilities, learning more and sharing the ideas I was managing to unveil and comprehend with respectful research. The understanding of the nature of spirits and their relations with men as well as the destine of the human race, the moral law and the immortality of the soul became for me peremptory, imperative, '*conditio sine qua non*' to spare relevant education not only for my own family and friends, but regarded these teachings as the very reason why humanity would choose life to death, peace to war, progress to aberrant convoluted behavior.

What classes I have taken or work places I have attended seem to be of little importance to share, now that you know where I am going. I function in the capacity of a knowledge seeker and a facilitator of information, indeed a philosopher and writer. Everything I receive as answers to my "never ending" questions I work diligently to share with as many people as possible hopping they will know how to listen wisely to only those types of information that are intrinsically capable to face logic and reason at all times and still remain consistent and coherent. I trust that you will follow but your heart and listen predominantly to your inner guidance.

Much love and progress with you and yours. I wish you enjoy this life time to become all you possibility can and teach others, by the clarity of your own examples, how to live by design. My heart of gratitude to you and all of those who will learn about this and any of my other books through you and your willingness to live fully YOUR highest excitement.

Here is the list I have very much enjoyed to write and share:

- Treb Bor yit-NE – Benevolent Hybrid Reptilian Humans (Co-authored with Rob Gauthier).
  Publication: November, 2011 – 480 pages.

- Insights with Adronis from Sirius - Adronis (Co-authored with Brad Johnson).
  Publication: October, 2011 – 354 pages.

- Feline Humans - Arvantis & The Arkoreuns (Co-authored with Shaun Swanson).
  Publication: March, 2010 – 296 pages.

- Avatars of the Phoenix Lights UFO - Ishuwa & The Yahyel (Co-authored with Shaun Swanson).
  Publication: March, 2012 – 292 pages.

- The Circle of Light & The Philosopher - Another magnificent day. (Co-authored with Georgia Jean).
  Publication: August 2010 – 213 pages.

A UNIVERSE OF POSSIBILITIES THAT AWAITS US ALL SILENTLY

A VERY "PALPABLE" CURIOSITY

Today is the 26th of October 2012. The way you can confirm we are "in the future" in regards to our book's last chapter of: October first, is by looking up the New York Times' front page: "Obama Campaign Endgame: Grunt Work and Cold Math." The fact I am aware that took place means it already happened. A couple of days ago, after having edited this book, I expressed to Rob Gauthier, the need to a last session with Treb Bor yit-NE his "guide" and our benevolent hybrid reptilian friend, to double check the name of each race and their respective planets to make sure we got everything down correctly and accordingly. It so happened that in the end of a free channeling consultation for a lady on the night of October 25th, before "disconnecting" Treb shared the following idea:

Lady: Okay! That makes better sense to me! And that will help me to move on where I have been kind of... uh... and wrap my mind around it, so thank you very much. Thank you very much!, also, for talking to me tonight. It has been really helpful to get the perspective on what happened on Monday in addition to the full searching that I have been doing today and that Terrence has been doing as well.

Treb Bor yit-NE: Yes! Before I disconnect, I wish to express an idea, that the host wish to speak. A man or an entity whose known to be Jefferson.

Lady: Okay, good!

Treb Bor yit-NE: The very first idea is the list of all entities, the planets in which they reside and the name of their races, according to what they have spoken. The **first** would be a one known to be Pit Lerone, from a planet that is known to be Hadmanee, and a race of those entities are called the Manila. The **second** idea is the one known to be Luluprakto. From a planet known to be the Plono and the race is named after the planet, which is also known to be Plono. The **third**, is the one entity known to be Kroyzep. The planet is known to be Zanetly. And the race is also known to be Zanetly. The **fourth** entity in which is called ProntLasForNotLasRecKitPla. Who is known to be from a planet called: the Soldrantee. And the race's name is known to be the Sanati. The **fifth** is the one who is known to be Haldra. For the planet there is no verbal representation made. So it has no given name. And the race is known to be Tranka. The **sixth** does not have a name but the name it represents is Sol and the name for the planet that he has chosen was the Soloid. And he did not give a specific name that he uses to represent his race. The **seventh** entity known to be Molgh Adier. Is from a planet which is known to be Drohn-Adier. And this is also named after the race for the Drohn-Adrier. The **next [eighth]** is from the entity known to be Tassasol. From a planet known to be FromAneel. From a race that is known to be the Kalamino. The **next [nineth]** entity is known to be I-o-solo. He is from a planet known to be Lad-i-nacee. From the Tinastola race. The **next [tenth]** entity is known to be SanJilKajone. From the Kistranah planet. From a race that is known to be the Sunaje Jepilso. The **next [eleventh]** entity is know to be QuilTravRiuposs. From the planet known to be Soulpions. And the race is named from the planet's, the Soulpions. And the **last [Twelveth]** entity is known to be

Extraterrestrial Life

Dwantilgo. From the planet called Quiltar. And the race's name is the Soulquantee. Uh... or perhaps the Soulquanty? Is the correct pronounciation of this? And I wish for you to represent this to the man which is known to be Jefferson so that he is very aware of these specific ideas. And with this I will leave you in love and in light and we will speak to each other or experience each other very soon.

*** The list below is what we have actually received from the races themselves as you can double check flipping back through each chapter since the titles were somewhat adjusted where we had no information for the race name or Planet. The order of placement is in accordance to the date of each connection.

Jefferson: First, 08/23/2012, Race: ? Humans. Planet Hadamanee. Spokesperson: P't Leronee. **Second**, 08/23/2012, Race: Plono Humans. Planet: Plono. Spokesperson: Luhluprahkto. **Third**, 08/23/2012, Race: Deasazonetly Humans Planet: Desazonetly. Spokesperson: Kroyzep. **Fourth**, 08/23/2012, Race: ? Humans Planet: Soldrantee. Spokesperson: Prontlasfornoplarecskitpla. **Fifth**, 09/05/2012, Race: Tranka Humans. Planet: [unpronounceable]. Spokesperson: Haldra. **Sixth,** 09/05/2012, Race: Sauloyd Humans Planet: Sauloyd. Spokesperson: Saul. **Seventh**, 09/06/2012, Race: ? Humans. Drohn-ondahg. Spokesperson: Mohj Ladrie. **Eighth**, 09/06/2012, Race: Kalameelo Humans Planet: FramAnehl. Spokesperson: Tassasol. **Nineth**, 09/07/2012, Race:? Humans Plante: KissTorNaoh. Spokesperson: SunjilKajone. **Tenth**, 09/07/2012, Race: SolePions Humans Planet: SolePion. Spokesperson: KwheelTravRiupaus. **Eleventh**, 09/12/2012, Race: Tihnas-Tolah Humans. Planet: Lahd-ieNacee; Spokesperson: Iosoma. **Twelveth**,

10/01/2012, Race: Sowkwanty Humans. Planet: Kwiltar. Spokesperson: Dwantelgo.

    If you are asking why I bothered to go over each detail is because our integrity, as responsible humans, demands from us that the information we read or share be funneled and filtered through the torches of logic and reason. In every channeled information consistency and the depth of content around the provided material is the best way to attest its validity as to assess its reality. Nobody wants to be deceived by an entity in embodiment or otherwise and nobody would be taken seriously as a representative of a knowledge based in hogwash. In every book I write and with each partner, I have but sought the qualities of honesty and spirit of service to others as well as engagement in discipline, simplicity from each medium and a certain sense of duty towards self and humanity from the interviewed extraterrestrial or spiritual entity.

    That said, I must advise you that like anything in such a dysfunctional society, no matter how careful you are, you can't get everything, every day, just perfect. So it will remain the responsibility of each one, who deal with any material of this nature, to be as refined as they want others to. A serious study is thus imperative to anyone who wishes to have a respected critique of such writings. And thus this "palpable" curiosity will provide those noble pathfinders, responsible go getters one more evidence of the reality behind these communication speaking tones to the existence of a universe of possibilities that awaits us all silently. Much perseverance in your inner struggles and I wish you take with you a renewed sense that you are not alone or forgotten, but unconditionally loved and oriented by those who live by design.

Jefferson Viscardi
October, 2012

We are grateful for this connection with your race
and with YOU personally through this book.

Thank you my friend!

We leave you for now in love and light.
Treb Bor yit-NE

Printed in Great Britain
by Amazon